Applying Psychology to Sport

Barbara Woods

APPLYING PSYCHOLOGY

to sport

BARBARA WOODS

Series Editor: **ROB McILVEEN**

Hodder & Stoughton

A MEMBER OF THE HODDER HEADLINE GROUP

Order: please contact Bookpoint Ltd, 130 Milton Park, Abingdon, Oxon OX14 4SB.
Telephone: (44) 01235 827720, Fax: (44) 01235 400454. Lines are open from 9.00 – 6.00, Monday to
Saturday, with a 24 hour message answering service. Email address: orders@bookpoint.co.uk

British Library Cataloguing in Publication Data
A catalogue record for this title is available from The British Library

ISBN 0 340 64760 4

First published 1998
Impression number   10   9   8   7   6   5
Year   2004 2003 2002

Copyright © 1998 Barbara Woods

Typeset by Transet Limited, Coventry, England
Printed in Great Britain for Hodder & Stoughton Educational, a division of Hodder Headline Plc,
338 Euston Road, London NW1 3BH by The Bath Press, Bath

CONTENTS

PREFACE

The aim of this book is to provide an introduction to sports psychology for those who are new to the topic. You may be an A level or an undergraduate student of sports studies, a sports coach, sportsperson or teacher of PE, but whatever your interest, I have assumed that you have no background in psychology. This book provides an introduction to some of the principles, theories and methods used in psychology whilst relating these to sports settings. My intention has been to help you understand the psychology behind suggestions and advice offered in coaching manuals or provided by teachers or trainers, so that you may be able to use and apply these principles in your own particular setting.

Research into sports psychology has expanded rapidly in the last 20 years, during which time it has changed in emphasis. Whereas earlier work tended to adapt psychological knowledge to sports setting, more recently theories have been generated by studying the athlete in the sports setting and this has provided new and fascinating material. Examples of this are research into competitive anxiety, self-efficacy and the affect of arousal on performance, which are all covered in this book.

The content of the book follows the content of the psychology component of the current AEB Sport Studies and PE syllabus. This includes both traditional areas of psychological study as well as the learning and control of motor skills. I hope that the diagrams, illustrations and photographs help you to understand the material, and that whatever your reason for reading this book, it increases your enjoyment of sport.

ACKNOWLEDGEMENTS

I would like to thank all those involved in the production of this book for their support, but particular thanks go to Anthony Curtis for valuable feedback and Kate Triscott for the supply of resources. As always, my greatest debt is to Richard for his encouragement both on and off the court.

chapter one

THE INDIVIDUAL IN SPORT

CHAPTER OVERVIEW

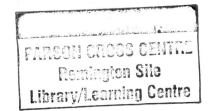
Why does someone prefer rock-climbing to hockey? Are there different reasons for competing? Why do marathon runners continue despite pain? Why do people want to improve their skills? Why don't we act in accordance with our beliefs? As individuals, we all know we are different from everyone else, yet we have many things in common with others. In this chapter we will look at some of the answers to these questions which psychologists have provided through their study of motivation, competitiveness, personality, attitudes and behaviour.

MOTIVATION

So why do people want to improve their skills? Why do marathon runners continue despite pain? In other words, what motivates people? Motivation has been seen as having two aspects: it is what drives us to do things (it *energises* our behaviour) and it makes us do particular things (it *directs* our behaviour). Some psychologists have seen motivation as due to arousal, and this view is discussed in detail in Chapter 4, Arousal, Anxiety and Stress in Performance. Here, we will examine proposals that motivation is a need, a personality trait or is due to reinforcement.

Motivation as need

Motivation has been described as the desire to fulfil a need. Abraham Maslow proposed that we all have a *hierarchy of needs*, the most basic being physiological needs such as food, and the highest needs being those related to self-fulfilment. This hierarchy is shown in Figure 1.1. Maslow (1954) argues that it is not until our basic needs have been at least partially satisfied that our higher needs become important. This means, for example, that a young player's needs for safety and comfort must be met to some extent before he is

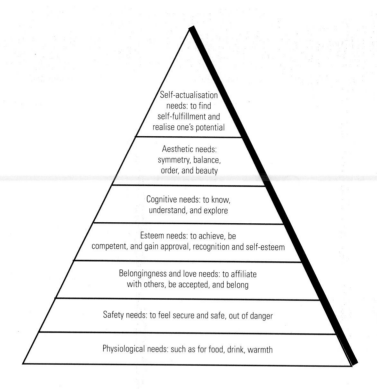

FIGURE 1.1 *Maslow's Hierarchy of Needs* (1954)

motivated to try to achieve or to understand. Maslow claimed that the highest motive – self-actualisation – can only be fulfilled after all other needs have been fulfilled. Participation in sports and exercise offers opportunities to fulfil these needs: it offers a *direction* for the fulfilment of the needs.

Achievement motivation

Achievement motivation is the individual's motivation to strive for success, which enables the individual to persist even when he or she meets obstacles and perhaps failure. This is a valuable quality in a sportsperson, which is why this area of psychology has been of interest. Imagine a young footballer in the last five minutes of a game in which the score is 1–1. He is asked if he wants to take the penalty kick. He considers he has a 50–50 chance of failing, imagines the shame of doing so and says 'No thanks'. His behaviour is driven by the *motive to avoid failure*. The next player who is asked thinks 'Hey, this is my chance to be a hero; I can save the match' and takes the penalty kick. He is driven by the *motive to achieve success*.

Atkinson (1964) saw achievement motivation as an aspect of personality, a stable disposition which is based on these two different motives. He proposed a theory of achievement motivation which took account of both the individual personality *and* the situation and specified how the two were related. Let us look at them in more detail.

The motive to achieve success

People with a high motive to achieve success show the following characteristics. They:

- look for challenges;
- are concerned about standards of excellence and show high levels of performance;
- persist for longer;
- value feedback from others;
- enjoy performing in situations in which they can be evaluated;
- are not afraid of failure;
- attribute their performance to internal factors: for example, success is due to effort, failure is due to poor concentration. For more on attribution, see p. 145.

The motive to avoid failure

People showing a strong motive to avoid failure tend to:

- be preoccupied about failure;
- avoid challenging tasks: for example, they prefer to play against very easy opposition (guaranteed success) or very difficult opposition (guaranteed failure which is not their fault);
- dislike situations in which there is a 50–50 chance of success and in which others can evaluate them, because this is the situation most likely to bring shame;
- perform worse when they can be evaluated by others;
- attribute their performance to external factors, for example success is due to luck, failure is due to tough opposition.

Although we all have these two motives to some extent, Atkinson proposes that it is the *difference* between the two motives which provides the personality factor called achievement motivation. So, in order to measure achievement motivation, the individual would be tested both for the motive to achieve success and for the motive to avoid failure. The larger the difference between the two scores, the greater the individual's achievement motivation.

Atkinson also considers the situation (or task) for the individual. If you recall our two young footballers, they responded differently to the same task – taking a penalty kick. They viewed the 50–50 chance of scoring a goal in different ways. There were two aspects to the task which determined their behaviour:

- **task difficulty:** the *probability* of success or of failure in the task;
- **incentive value of success:** the *importance* to the individual of success or failure in the task.

FIGURE 1.2 *Arwell Thomas preparing to take a match-saving conversion (Wales v Scotland in 1966). He fails to convert*

Atkinson proposed that it was possible to identify whether people were high or low in achievement motivation by asking them to choose between two types of task. Research showed that high achievers prefer to do a task with a 50 per cent chance of success, such as playing an opponent of similar ability at table-tennis. Low achievers prefer to do either a very easy (certain success) or very difficult (certain failure) task. This means that they would prefer to play against a very weak or very strong opponent. Research has also shown that, if possible, low achievers prefer to avoid *all* challenges, whereas high achievers prefer to play the club champion than no-one at all.

Evaluation of Atkinson's theory

Although research has shown that those classed as high achievers prefer risky and challenging situations and that the choice of task with a 50 per cent chance of success is a useful indicator of achievement motivation, there have been a number of criticisms of Atkinson's theory. These include:

- **measuring achievement motivation**: a major concern is that assessment methods (such as asking participants to report their attitudes or using anxiety scales) have proved to be unreliable measures;
- **calculating achievement motivation**: it is not clear how the scores for each motive should be interpreted, for example when analysing results, the scores have been ignored when they are from participants for whom neither motive seems particular strong;
- **achievement motivation and performance**: it appears that there is no clear relationship between achievement motivation and level of performance, because research findings on this topic are often contradictory;
- **achievement motivation is a 'global' concept**: because the term is used to cover achievement in general, some psychologists have proposed that it would be more useful to break down the concept of achievement motivation. For example, an individual may be highly motivated to achieve success in gymnastics but not in singing. This has led sports psychologists to talk of sport-specific achievement motivation – in other words, *competitiveness*.

Competitiveness

We have just considered the motive to achieve success and the motive to avoid failure. Martens (1976) proposed that in a sports setting these are:

- **competitive trait anxiety**, which is the motive to avoid failure in sport competition: research on this topic has advanced considerably and it is discussed in more detail in Chapter 4, Arousal, Anxiety and Stress in Sports Performance, p. 99;
- **competitiveness**, which is the motive to approach success in sport competition: research on competitiveness has proved more difficult; nevertheless, the Sport Orientation Questionnaire (SOQ) was developed by Gill and Deeter (1988) to measure competitiveness and competitive behaviours. It is comprised of 25 questions which together measure three dimensions:

1 **competitiveness**: the desire to seek and strive for success in sport-specific situations;
2 **win orientation**: the desire to win interpersonal competitive sporting events;
3 **goal orientation**: the desire to reach personal goals in sport.

Research using the SOQ has compared athletes and non-athletes, and male and female athletes. Results showed that:

- males consistently scored higher than females on competitiveness and win orientation;
- females generally scored a little higher on goal orientation;
- athletes scored higher than non-athletes on most dimensions of the SOQ;
- athletes were more concerned about performance and less about outcome than non-athletes.

How does achievement motivation develop?

According to White (1959), we are born with a *competence motive*, which is the need to confirm our sense of personal competence. This need motivates us to explore our environment and learn how to deal effectively with it because it is intrinsically rewarding and satisfying to feel that we are capable human beings, able to understand, predict and control our world. You can see where the competence motive appears on Maslow's Hierarchy of Needs (see p. 2)

Competence motivation can be seen even in very young children as they explore, try to grasp or push. It develops as they set themselves goals and try to reach those goals. A two year old who struggles to heave all his toys into a large box is just like an elite athlete: he has set himself a goal which he is striving to achieve. Veroff (1969) has proposed that *achievement motivation* develops in a sequence of three stages, and this has implications particularly for those who coach young children.

1 **Autonomous competence stage**. Up to about five years of age, the child is most concerned with mastering skills. The two year old will repeat the same actions again and again, doing the same jigsaw, piling things up, repeatedly jumping off the stairs. She is not really interested in whether someone else can jump further or pile things higher; she rarely compares herself with others, her concern is to do better than she did last time. She uses internal standards; she sets herself a goal, tries to achieve it and evaluates her efforts.
2 **Social comparison stage**. From about six years old, the child not only notices others, but starts to compare herself with others: who is the tallest, fastest, strongest. The child's focus is on herself in comparison with others: these are external standards. She is unlikely to progress to the next stage of development if she is uncomfortable in competitive situations or if she undertakes competition mainly to beat others and to satisfy her own ego. However, if she enjoys competitive situations and uses them to gain feedback about her own skills and learn from others, she is likely to progress.
3 **Integrated stage**. There is no fixed age for this; it depends on the child's maturation, experiences and her understanding of them. This is reached when the individual uses both internal and external (or social) standards to evaluate her performance and knows when it is appropriate to use each one.

APPLICATION
The coach's role when working with children

There is little point in setting up competitive situations for the under 5s, but their fascination with mastery can be put to good use in helping them develop basic skills such as balancing, throwing, catching and running. For nine year olds, the problem is to keep them interested without using competitive situations too much! They tend to be outcome orientated – to focus on winning. The coach's role is to help them focus on setting their own targets for their own improvements – to become goal orientated.

Intrinsic and extrinsic motivation

Alternative explanations for motivation come from learning theory (see p. 67). This says that a behaviour is more likely to be repeated if it is rewarded, so it is the reward that motivates the behaviour. If a reward comes from *outside* the individual (such as praise), then it is known as extrinsic motivation. In contrast, the satisfaction of improving your best lap time comes from *inside* yourself. Thus, satisfaction is an example of intrinsic motivation.

The distinction between the two types of motivation is important because they work in different ways and have a different effect on the individual's attitude and success in physical activities.

Intrinsic motivation

The 40-year-old who takes up marathon running and trains three nights a week and Sundays is likely to be motivated by intrinsic rewards such as improved well-being or the satisfaction of a faster finishing time, rather than by the extrinsic reward of the winner's medal. Intrinsic motivation depends on the athlete's own attitudes and perceptions and therefore involves the athlete's cognitions, or understanding of their circumstances.

Deci (1975) proposed that behaviours which are intrinsically motivating are:

'those which a person engages in to feel competent and self-determining' (p.61).

So, intrinsic motivation is different from extrinsic motivation because it arises spontaneously – it does not have to be provided by others. According to this view, intrinsic motivation is, like any drive, never fully satisfied, so the individual will continue to seek out opportunities to satisfy these needs. This

FIGURE 1.3a   Trophies provide extrinsic motivation

FIGURE 1.3b   This young player's pleasure provides him with intrinsic motivation

means that intrinsic motivation can be very persistent and it should therefore be the aim of every coach to encourage the development of intrinsic, as opposed to extrinsic, motivation.

Extrinsic motivation

By its very nature, sport provides many forms of extrinsic rewards. They may be concrete, such as a trophy, or intangible, for example prestige or praise (which are also known as social reinforcements). They can act as motivators, making the individual more likely to perform the behaviours which are being rewarded, as the research below shows.

RESEARCH
Smith, Smoll and Curtis (1979)

The researchers compared children whose coaches gave frequent encouragement and reinforcement when mistakes were corrected with those whose coaches did not show these behaviours. They found that the children who were given encouragement reported greater enjoyment and enthusiasm for the coming season than children who were not. In addition, the 'positive' approach had the most dramatic impact on children who started with lowest levels of self-esteem.

Extrinsic motivation (reinforcement) must be carefully used, it should be:

- **appropriate to the individual**: for example, consider two swimmers who have just achieved a personal best time; one may be delighted at public praise from his coach, the other might prefer a quiet pat on the back to the embarrassment of public praise;
- **given as a result of particular behaviours**: for example, to provide feedback about correct footwork;
- **given as soon as possible after the behaviour occurs**, in order that the association between the behaviour (correct footwork) and the reinforcement ('Nice footwork there!') is strong;
- **applied intermittently and gradually phased out** so that the behaviour continues without extrinsic rewards: according to the principles of learning theory, behaviour which is continually rewarded will stop when the rewards are removed (see p. 67, for more details).

However, if rewards are used excessively or inappropriately, they can demotivate. For instance, if everyone on the team is rewarded equally, this reduces the effectiveness of the reward for the individual. Excessive use of rewards may also be seen as a form of bribe, which may be resented.

Extrinsic motivation is therefore useful to identify and encourage the performance of correct skills, moves and behaviour.

The relationship between intrinsic and extrinsic motivation

Both intrinsic and extrinsic rewards can increase motivation. We would therefore expect that if we gave an extrinsic reward (such as a trophy) to someone who was already intrinsically motivated to improve performance, this should produce even higher levels of motivation. However, it seems that extrinsic motivation may *damage* intrinsic motivation and lead to a decrease in performance, as the research described below suggests.

RESEARCH
Lepper and Greene (1975)

Observers noted the amount of free time children in a nursery spent drawing with felt pens – an intrinsically rewarding activity. This enabled researchers to establish a base-line time. After this some of the children were promised a 'good player' certificate for drawing with the pens, each was later given a certificate. The children in another group were each given the certificate after drawing for the researcher, but they had not been told they would get it. Those in the final group were neither promised nor received certificates after they had drawn with the pens. One week later, the children were again observed to see how long they played with the pens, and observations showed that the group who had been promised and received certificates spent less playing time than before. There was no difference in the playing times for the children in the other two groups.

So, a golfer who takes the sport up for the pleasure of developing skills is intrinsically motivated. If a coach praises every correct execution of a new shot, the golfer may start to devalue the activity and become less motivated to continue. Deci (1975) proposed that extrinsic motivation can provide information and be interpreted as a form of control. Extrinsic motivation can therefore affect intrinsic motivation in the following ways.

- **confidence**: the information provided by extrinsic rewards may enhance or damage intrinsic motivation because it affects our feelings of competence. When someone receives a reward for achievement this provides evidence of their competence and increases self-confidence. This in turn increases intrinsic motivation. However, failing to achieve something you have worked for might reduce your confidence and thus have a damaging effect on intrinsic motivation.
- **control**: we do things because we want to but when extrinsic rewards are applied, we may feel we are being controlled by others. The controlling

aspect of rewards conflicts with our need to be self-determining. If we do not feel that the reward is controlling our behaviour, then it will not affect intrinsic motivation.

■ **competition**: competing may also reduce motivation and, though *performance* may increase, intrinsic motivation may *decrease*, as research by Deci and his colleagues shows.

RESEARCH
Deci et al. (1981)

This study looked at the effect of competition. Half of the participants were given an interesting task alongside others and told to try to beat the others. The other half were not given these instructions to compete. All the participants were allowed to 'win' in the tasks. However, later on when participants had a choice of activities to pursue, there was less motive to continue the same task for those who had been in the 'competitive' situation, and this was particularly true for females.

Extrinsic rewards such as the achievement awards (Teddy Bear, Tadpole and Frog) operated by the Swimming Teachers Association can be valuable motivators. Positive comments from others ('good pass') provide extrinsic motivation as well as information to the sportsperson about his or her performance. These help evaluate performance and thus increase the individual's sense of competence, which provides intrinsic motivation. However too much emphasis on rewards can damage motivation and participation, so they should be used with caution as shown in the application described below.

APPLICATION
Using extrinsic and intrinsic motivation

A child takes up tennis because she is intrigued by watching it on TV. During early sessions, the coach gives a low level of encouragement because the child's own interest is intrinsically motivating and the coach does not want to reduce this. However, the coach gives explicit praise for her correct execution of a forehand stroke. This extrinsic motivation also provides feedback to the child and helps her to develop the correct skills. The coach provides the opportunity for the child to use these skills successfully, such as by feeding easy forehand shots in a game so that she experiences feelings of mastery and competence. These are intrinsic rewards and will motivate the child to continue to play and improve, without extrinsic reinforcement from the coach.

PERSONALITY AND SPORT

Earlier in this chapter, we looked at the view that competitiveness can be seen as a personality trait. So is there an 'athletic personality'? One study of international athletes found that they shared several personality traits. They were more self-confident, competitive and socially outgoing than non-athletes (Cooper, 1969). Does this mean young athletes with these traits are more likely to be successful than those without them? Not necessarily, for example, in a study of sport's highest achievers, David Hemery (1986) reported that of the 63 international athletes he interviewed, 89 per cent of them said they were initially shy and introverted.

FIGURE 1.4 *Duncan Goodhew (left) described himself as an introvert who had been made to feel self-conscious because of his dyslexia. Steve Cram (right) said sport had brought him out, he became more assertive after winning*

So, does personality predict success? Can sports participation change personality traits? Do particular traits direct the individual towards a type of sport? These are the kind of questions which sports psychologists have tried to answer as they examine the role of personality in participation, motivation, performance and choice of sport.

Definitions of personality

First we need to clarify what is meant by personality. All individuals operate in a social environment: Hollander (1971) showed personality as a structure with a core, a middle and an outer layer which is affected by the social environment surrounding it. This is shown in Figure 1.5. The outer layer is closest to, and therefore most affected by, the social environment, whereas the core is protected from the social environment and is therefore largely unchanging.

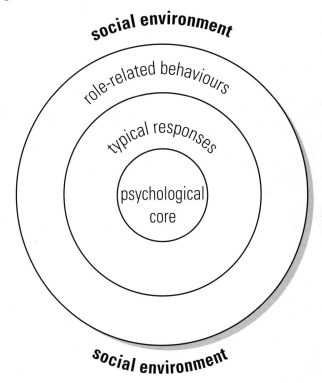

FIGURE 1.5 *The structure of personality (from Hollander, 1971)*

The characteristics of each layer are:

■ **the core**: the psychological core is the centre of the personality, including the individual's self-concept, basic attitudes and values; these qualities are seen as being relatively permanent;

- **the middle**: this comprises the typical responses, which are the usual way in which we respond to situations, such as being fouled or winning a difficult match; these typical responses indicate the individual's psychological core because they are the way in which he or she *usually* responds to situations;
- **the outer**: the role-related behaviour is the outer part of our personalities and depends on the circumstances we are in; because they are constantly changing, this the most changeable part of personality, and may bear little relationship to the psychological core.

It may be useful to think of personality in this way, but it does not tell us what personality is. Hollander's (1971) definition is that it is:

'the sum total of the individual's characteristics which make him unique.' (p. 394)

This reflects one aspect of personality on which psychologists tend to agree – that it is unique to the individual – but they differ about how stable it is over time, how it is related to behaviour and how and when it is affected by the environment.

Those who see personality as a core of fairly stable traits emphasise the role of these traits in explaining and predicting behaviour. On the other hand, there are psychologists who argue that behaviour is determined mostly by the situation the individual is in – thus we need to know the situation before we can understand and predict an individual's behaviour. Below we consider both trait and situation explanations for personality before we go on to look at a third alternative – the interactional approach.

The trait approach

Trait theories propose that personality can be described in terms of a limited number of traits which we all have, but to varying degrees. These traits are long lasting and stable; they cause us to behave in characteristic ways. They are therefore frequently evident in the individual's behaviour, and knowing these traits will enable us to explain and predict that person's behaviour.

Eysenck's theory

Hans Eysenck (1955) proposed from his research that there are a considerable number of personality traits which, because they are related to each other, can be grouped together in two ways. Eysenck called these two *dimensions* of personality and asserted that these dimensions have a biological basis. We will look first at the biological basis and characteristics of these dimensions before we move on to examine how Eysenck assesses an individual on these dimensions.

- **Extrovert – introvert dimension** (called E): – Eysenck argues that human beings seek to maintain a level of stimulation or activation which is comfortable for them. Activation is directed by the reticular activating system (the RAS). However, the level of activation which the individual finds comfortable varies from person to person. This variation is identified in the E dimension (Table 1.1).

Table 1.1 The biological basis and characteristics of Eysenck's extrovert–introvert dimension of personality

	Extrovert	Introvert
Biological basis	RAS dampens down incoming information so the individual seeks additional stimulation in order to maintain a comfortable level of activation	RAS amplifies incoming information so the individual prefers low levels of stimulation in order to avoid excessive activation.
Characteristics	becomes bored more quickly is less responsive to pain seeks change and excitement is poor at tasks requiring concentration	does not seek excitement, prefers calm and quiet dislikes the unexpected, prefers order is good at tasks requiring concentration

- **Stable – neurotic dimension** (called N): Eysenck's N dimension is associated with emotionality. Its physiological basis is the autonomic nervous system (the ANS), in particular how rapidly the autonomic nervous system responds to stressful situations (Table 1.2).

Table 1.2 The biological basis and characteristics of Eysenck's stable–neurotic dimension of personality

	Stable	Neurotic
Biological basis	ANS is fairly slow to respond to stressful situations and is not very vigorous	ANS responds rapidly and strongly to stressful situations
Characteristics	even-tempered emotionally stable easy going	restless excitable anxious

The Eysenck Personality Inventory (Eysenck and Eysenck, 1964) asks respondents a number of questions, such as whether they daydream a lot or find it hard to say no. Each question requires a yes or no answer, a score is calculated from the answers and the individual's position on each dimension can then be established. Eysenck proposed that most people would score about the middle of each dimension, with very few being at either end. Both these dimensions are independent of each other, so it is possible to find a stable introvert and a stable extrovert. Particular personality traits are associated with high scores on each dimension, as can be seen in Figure 1.6.

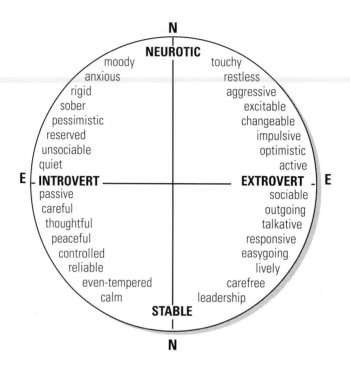

FIGURE 1.6 *Eysenck's dimensions of personality (1965)*

Eysenck proposed that 75 per cent of the basis for these traits is due to genetic influence, and 25 per cent is due to environmental influence. In other words, it is quite difficult to change or modify these personality traits.

The use of Eysenck's theory in sport

What is the relevance of these dimensions to sport? On the E dimension, introverts were found to be well-represented amongst distance runners (Morgan and Costill 1972), and Eysenck et al. (1982) proposed that extroverts are more attracted to action-orientated sports such as football, which give the frequent stimulus they need. They also claim that people scoring at the stable end of the N dimension were more likely to be found amongst athletes than amongst the general population. Athletes at the neurotic end of the dimension are already high in arousal. They are likely to experience over-arousal as they prepare to compete and this may impede performance, whereas the emotionally stable athlete will be less likely to be affected. (See Chapter 4, where the relationship between arousal and performance is considered in much more detail). The Profile of Mood States (see p. 21) reflects this finding as it indicates that successful athletes tend to show lower levels of tension than unsuccessful athletes.

Cattell's theory: 16 personality factors

Cattell believed that personality consists of a number of traits (or personality factors) which we all show to some degree and he devised the 16PF questionnaire to measure how much of each trait a person shows (Cattell, 1965). Individuals can then be placed at a point on the range 1 – 10 for each of the 16 personality factors to give their personality profile, as shown in Figure 1.7. Cattell claims that the 16PF provides more detailed information than Eysenck's Personality Inventory, though he does not claim that individuals will show similar scores each time they complete the 16PF questionnaire. He acknowledges that influences such as mood, motivation and situational factors will affect responses.

	Low score description	Average	High score description
A	reserved, cool, impersonal		warm, easygoing, likes people
B	concrete-thinking		abstract-thinking
C	easily upset, emotional, impatient		emotionally stable
E	submissive, accommodating		dominant, assertive, opinionated
F	serious, sober, prudent, quiet		cheerful, expressive, enthusiastic
G	expedient, disregards rules		conforming, persevering, rule-bound
H	shy, timid, threat-sensitive		socially bold, unafraid, can take stress
I	tough-minded, insensitive, rough		sensitive, tender-minded, refined
L	trusting, adaptable, accepting		suspicious, hard-to-fool, sceptical
M	practical, "down to earth", conventional		imaginative, absent-minded, impractical
N	forthright, unpretentious, open		shrewd, polished, calculating
O	confident, self-satisfied, complacent		insecure, apprehensive, self-blaming
Q_1	conservative, traditional, resists change		liberal, innovative, open to change
Q_2	group-oriented, sociable		self-sufficient, resourceful, self-directed
Q_3	undisciplined, uncontrolled, impulsive		controlled, socially precise, compulsive
Q_4	relaxed, composed, has lower drive		tense, restless, has high drive

FIGURE 1.7 *The 16 personality factors in the 16PF (from Cattell, 1965)*

From analysis of these 16 personality factors, Cattell claimed there were a number of 'second order' factors, two of which reflect Eysenck's E and N dimensions. Cattell labelled them *exvia–invia* and *anxiety*.

The use of Cattell's theory in sport

Cattell's 16PF has been widely used in sports research. For example, Kroll and Crenshaw (1970) compared the personality profiles of highly skilled participants in American football, wrestling, gymnastics and karate using the 16PF. They found the wrestlers and football players had similar personality profiles, but those involved in gymnastics and karate differed from each other, as well as from the football players and wrestlers.

Another study aimed to identify whether personality was related to the level of skill a player could achieve. The personality profiles of male hockey players at international, national and club standard were compared using Cattell's 16PF. Results showed that the internationals differed significantly from the club players, but the national players could not be distinguished from either of the other two groups (Williams and Parkin, 1980).

Evaluation of trait theories

These theories created considerable interest amongst psychologists, and led to research and later revisions by Eysenck and by Cattell. Nevertheless, there are criticisms, some related to the weaknesses of personality tests in general (which are detailed later in this chapter, see p. 23) but others are specific to the trait approach. These are that:

- trait approaches see personality traits as more fixed and long lasting than they really are (for example, the profile generated by Catell's 16PF is likely to vary over time, as he recognised)
- they do not take account of the *understanding* individuals have of themselves (their cognition).
- they fail to account for the effect of a *situation* on an individual's behaviour or attitudes (the situational view). Catell acknowledged that a different situation may lead to a different profile, but the 16PF cannot explain this.
- trait approaches have been useful in helping to explain why people choose particular sports, but have been less useful in predicting success.

By the early 1980s, sports psychologists were divided about the value of using personality tests to predict performance. There were two views:

- **the credulous view** was that generally personality tests were accurate predictors of athletic success;
- **the sceptical view** was that personality tests were of little value in predicting athletic success.

Nevertheless, the view developed that personality was a useful indicator but should be considered together with physiological and situational factors in order to be of real value in predicting success. The role of situational factors began to receive much more attention from psychologists, as can been seen in social learning theory.

The situational approach: social learning theory

The social learning view of personality is that it is not a stable core, but that it is built up out of our experiences in the social world. Walter Mischel (1968) reviewed work on personality and concluded that there was little evidence that people behaved consistently in a variety of situations – their behaviour varies depending on the *situation* (or environment) they are in. The following quotation (from Hemery, 1986) is about Bryan Robson, Captain of Manchester United and England in the 1980's, and shows that his assertiveness depended on the situation he was in:

> 'He was happy to give instructions and take command on the field, but off the field he was quite the opposite. "I walk away from people in pubs or restaurants who are making uncalled-for remarks, trying to set me up for a fight".' (p. 55)

Mischel argues that we see patterns and consistency in the behaviour of others where none exists because we all try to impose some stability and predictability on our experiences. From the situationist point of view, personality is the behaviours we show, and these result from our experiences or the roles we play, not from a biological predisposition or core.

The basis of social learning theory is that we learn through two types of experience – modelling and reinforcement. As we grow up, we observe what other people do, and we may imitate (or model) their behaviour. In addition, if we are rewarded (reinforced) when we do something, we are likely to repeat it. Albert Bandura (1977b) proposed that we are more likely to model people who are powerful or similar to us, for example someone of the same sex. For more details on learning by observation see p. 69.

Bandura identified four stages in the process of observational learning. We can look at each stage to see how it relates to the personality of a ten-year-old boy who is keen on tennis. He is watching the men's semi-finals at Wimbledon. Both players may become models for the boy because he sees them as powerful (well known, on TV) and similar to him (tennis players, male). One player has lost the first two sets and is behind in the third and the youngster pays particular attention to the losing player because he too knows what it feels like to be in this losing situation. The four stages are:

1 **attention**: the boy notices how this player spends a few moments with his eyes closed and body relaxed. He comes out for the next game looking very controlled. His stance shows confidence, his facial expression shows intense concentration, he goes on to win the set.

2 **retention**: the boy remembers the player's relaxed posture and subsequent confident approach, as well as his success in winning the set.
3 **motor reproduction**: the next time the youngster is in a losing situation he imitates this behaviour, sitting with his eyes closed, trying to appear relaxed, and then he goes on court looking confident.
4 **motivational response**: if he feels more confident and improves his game when he behaves in this way, this rewards his behaviour and makes him more likely to repeat it. In this way he develops feelings of self-efficacy about his tennis; he will behave with confidence.

The social learning view sees the individual's personality developing in this way as a result of observing the behaviours of others, paying attention, reproducing the behaviours of significant others and continuing to do so if those behaviours are rewarded. If they are not, then the behaviour will not be established. Mischel's (1968) point is that the boy's confident behaviour may only be apparent in tennis; he may continue to lack confidence in maths, for example. It is the situation (playing tennis), not his personality, which is the main determinant of his behaviour.

Evaluation of the situational approach

Although this explanation counteracts the trait theorist view of personality as fairly permanent and stable, critics argue it goes too far in the opposite direction. In other words, they argue that there is some consistency in the individual's behaviour over time and in a variety of circumstances, which the situational approach fails to account for.

The interactional approach

This approach to the understanding of personality can explain more of our behaviour than traits or situations alone, according to Bowers (1973). It is particularly interesting to sports psychologists because of the extreme situations which sportspeople put themselves into. For example, they may experience particularly high levels of stress (competition), of boredom (training), of disappointment (losing, injury), of risk (rock-climbing), of dependence on others (team sports).

The interactional approach takes into account personal factors, the situation in which behaviour occurs, and the interaction of these two factors. It predicts that:

- when situational factors are strong, they are more likely than personality factors to affect behaviour. A player who is usually fairly calm may explode with delight on finally winning a close and crucial match. This exhibition is uncharacteristic, a response to this particular situation (see Fig. 1.8).
- when situational factors are not strong, personality is more likely to affect behaviour.

FIGURE 1.8 *Stefan Edberg, who was usually calm, shows an uncharacteristic response*

The difficulty is: how can situational and personality factors be separated and measured? One technique used by psychologists is known as the trait–state approach, and has been used particularly to analyse anxiety in sportspeople. If a coach can identify how much of a competitor's pre-competition anxiety is due to personality factors (the individual), and how much is due to the imminent competition (the situation), the coach should be able to help the sportsperson cope with anxiety and turn it to the best possible use.

Taking the interactional view, the coach can also study the way individuals act in particular settings, for example by asking rugby players to assess their level of anxiety in a number of different play situations – kicking to convert a try, missing a conversion, dropping the ball, criticism by a respected team member. The coach can identify which situations the player finds most anxiety provoking and plan accordingly. For a detailed discussion of both trait anxiety and state anxiety, and ways of measuring them, see Chapter 4, Arousal, Anxiety and Stress in Performance, p. 98.

Profile of Mood States

The study of competitive anxiety is an example of the interest in psychological *states*: that is, the mood which is temporarily created by being in a particular situation. The Profile of Mood States (POMS), devised by McNair, Lorr and Droppleman (1971), was designed to measure the following mood states:

tension : depression : anger : vigour : fatigue : confusion

Morgan (1979) compared successful elite athletes with unsuccessful athletes and results showed a difference in their scores on each of the above moods. Elite athletes produced an 'iceberg profile', which is shown in Figure 1.9.

We can see from Figure 1.9 that whereas unsuccessful athletes show a similar score for all moods (which produces a fairly level line), the successful athlete's score on 'vigour' is well *above* that of the unsuccessful athlete, but scores on other moods (tension, depression, fatigue, confusion) are well *below* those of the unsuccessful athlete. The successful athlete thus scores higher on the positive mood and lower on the negative moods. Research shows wide support for the iceberg profile, for example in female long-distance runners (Morgan et al, 1987b) and triathlon athletes (Bell and Howe, 1988).

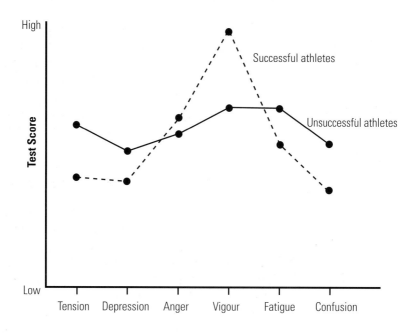

FIGURE 1.9 *Scores for athletes on the POMS showing the iceberg profile (adapted from Morgan, 1979)*

However, this does not always hold true. Morgan et al. (1987a) reviewed POMS scores for swimmers when they were undergoing training. Results showed that as the training demands became heavier, there were changes in the swimmers' moods. Swimmers who were overtrained showed the *opposite* pattern: their vigour *decreased* and the negative mood states of tension, depression and fatigue *increased*. The coach can reduce the effect of over-training by changing the structure of the regime or setting different goals. (See Chapter 3, Learning and Teaching Skills, p. 75, for more on practices and training.)

The use of personality tests in sport settings

We have seen that personality tests have frequently been used for research purposes and they do have a role to play in a sports setting, but there are some important points to keep in mind, which are discussed below.

- Validity: the test should measure what it claims to measure. As there is no agreed definition of personality or mood, how can we know what these terms mean and how can we be confident that is what we are measuring? For example, if the tests provide accurate measures of permanent traits, then behaviour should be consistent with the traits identified. Though research has provided some evidence of this, as we have seen above, there are still conflicting results.
- Reliability: the tests should produce similar results when repeated. Though this appears to be true for Eysenck's test, Cattell himself acknowledged that the same people would produce different profiles at different times, depending on their mood and so on. Thus, the 16PF does not have good reliability.
- The self-report questionnaire method has weaknesses because respondents' answers may be affected by, for example, their mood, attitude to tests or the person giving the test.
- Respondents may not answer accurately or honestly, although Eysenck included a lie scale in his EPI to measure the individual's tendency to give socially desirable answers.
- This approach to the study of personality is rather limited, for example Eysenck's EPI asks only for 'yes or no' answers. Although tests can give us insights into behaviour, they are not good predictors of attitudes, success, motivation or skills, all of which play a crucial part in participation and successful performance. Thus, personality tests should not be the only basis for making decisions, selections or predictions about the athlete.
- Tests should be conducted with regard to ethics. Personality testing is a sensitive process and testers should not probe beyond what is necessary. The athlete's permission must be given and the full details of what is involved and the purpose of the test must be explained. Results of the test are confidential and the athlete's permission must be gained before results can be given to anyone else. The tester should be qualified to administer and interpret the test results.

ATTITUDES: THEIR ROLE IN SPORT

Psychologists who study attitudes are interested in how they affect behaviour, and how they can be changed. This is of particular concern to those working in physical education and sport because they wish to create and maintain positive attitudes so that people will be encouraged to participate, persist in their efforts and achieve more. Attitudes can be positive, negative or neutral. For example:

- A middle-aged man watches the London marathon on TV and notices the variety of people who participate – some are his age and others do not look very fit. He sees the encouragement they give each other as well as their delight at finishing and thinks he might have a go next year; he has a positive attitude.
- The man's brother, who is also watching, notices that runners look ill, some are collapsing, others have bandaged knees, no-one notices when they finish. He cannot really see the point of it all; he has a negative attitude.

The formation of attitudes

Where do attitudes come from? How are they formed? They develop from a variety of sources: as a result of our experiences in school and with our friends; the outcome of our own efforts at sports activities; what our parents, teachers or friends say and do; by sports stars and the way the media present sports stories.

- **Positive attitudes** tend to form towards things with which we are familiar or which are easily available. For example, children are more likely to form a positive attitude to an activity which their parents pursue (karate), or which is played frequently at school (netball), which is easy to play informally (football), or which is shown on TV (golf). Availability gives the child the opportunity to try out these skills and enjoy success, again increasing positive attitudes. Being exposed to the positive attitudes of others, particularly those we like or admire, helps us form positive attitudes to the same things.
- **A negative attitude** may result if someone has an unpleasant experience. For example, if a child is struck by a hockey stick and suffers painful bruising, he or she may be put off playing again. This attitude may then extend to other sports with a higher risk of injury. Failure in sports can also create negative attitudes, such as when players feel they are not making progress or are letting the rest of the team down.

The three parts of attitude

Attitudes can be seen as having three parts. Look at Triandis' (1971) definition:

> 'ideas charged with emotion (positive or negative) which pre-disposes a class of actions to a particular social situation.' (p.2)

This incorporates the three parts of attitude: ideas (or cognitions), emotions (also called affects) and actions (or behaviour). Let us look at each of these by considering a PE teacher who has girls and boys attending soccer training. He may think that the girls are more likely to drop out than the boys, he may be unenthusiastic about having them involved and focuses his attention on the boys. The three parts (known as the ABC of attitude) are:

- **affective** (feelings or emotions): the teacher is unenthusiastic about girls in football;
- **behavioural** (actions): the teacher discriminates against girls in his training sessions and team selection;
- **cognitive** (ideas, knowledge, beliefs): the teacher thinks girls are more likely to drop out than boys.

By breaking the attitude down like this it is possible to see what the cause of behaviour might be and how we might be successful in changing the attitude. However, the relationship between attitudes and behaviour is not quite so simple.

The relationship between attitudes and behaviour

A major problem is that we do not always act in accordance with what we think or what we feel. Imagine that our PE teacher knows about the self-fulfilling prophecy: this predicts that if you have an expectation about someone and treat them accordingly, they will act in the way you expected. As a good teacher, he will ensure that he *treats* girls just the same as boys, even though he *thinks* the girls will soon drop out. In other words, his behaviour conflicts with his beliefs.

This relates to another difficulty: frequently we do not know another person's attitude so we *infer* it from that person's behaviour or appearance. For example, a rugby coach notices that one of his young players turns up late for pre-training warm-ups and thinks the player's attitude to warm-up sessions is that they are not much use and he dislikes them. The player may in fact know that warm-ups are crucial to successful play but he avoids them because he lacks confidence in his speed on the rugby pitch: he uses lack of warm-up as an excuse to justify poor play. In other words, the player's *behaviour* is not in accordance with his *attitude* to warm-ups.

Research has shown that the relationship between behaviour and attitude is affected by the following factors:

- **The importance** of the attitude to the individual: the more important the attitude is to the individual, the more likely it is that behaviour will be consistent with it (if the PE teacher's commitment to equality of opportunity is important to him, then it is likely that his behaviour will reflect this attitude).
- **The strength** of the attitude: the stronger it is, the more consistent the behaviour (if the rugby player's participation in warm-up sessions increases when a major competitive event is near, we might conclude that this player's attitude to warm-ups is not very strongly held).
- **The degree of control** over the behaviour: the more we feel able to do something, have the opportunities or resources to do it, the more likely it is that our behaviour will reflect our attitudes (the TV viewer described earlier in this section, who had a positive attitude to marathon running, will be more likely to participate in next year's event if he knows someone he can train with and has the time to prepare for it).

Measuring attitudes

Psychologists have devised various ways to measure attitudes to help them discover what attitudes are held and how strongly they are held. There are a number of ways of measuring attitudes, such as by observing what people do (for example body language) or measuring physiological responses (for example heart rate and other measures related to stress). More popular techniques include interviews or using *attitude scales*.

An attitude scale could be used, for example, to measure someone's attitude to aggression in sport. To do this, a number of statements about aggression will be devised. This list (which is called an attitude scale) is given to the individual, who is asked to respond to each statement, and from these responses a measure of the individual's attitude can be calculated. Let us see how this works in the three attitude scales which we will look at now – the Thurstone, Likert and Osgood scales.

Thurstone Scale (1931)

A large number of statements (called items) are written which express a range of attitudes about the topic being investigated, going from positive to negative. The statements should be short and easily understood, for example 'Aggression adds to the excitement of sport' or 'Referees should be tougher on aggressive behaviour'. Then a panel of judges is asked to give each item a score on a scale of 1 to 11. Those items for which the scores vary widely are rejected until there are 11 favourable and 11 unfavourable items left – these items make up the attitude scale. The mean (average) score for each of them is noted, and called the scale value.

The scale value indicates how the judges rate the statement, so a score value of 6 indicates a neutral statement because it is half-way between 1 and 11.

'Aggression adds to the excitement of sport' may have a score value of 9, showing that it is a statement that is favourable towards aggression in sport. 'Referees should be tougher on aggressive behaviour' may have a scale value of 3, indicating a statement judged as unfavourable to aggression in sport.

The person completing the attitude scale (called the respondent) is asked to tick every statement he or she agrees with and the score values on each ticked statement are added together. The average (or mean value) is calculated by dividing the total score by the number of statements ticked; this gives the respondent's attitude score.

The Thurstone Scale does provide a way of discovering an individual's attitude in comparison to others. However, it is also expensive and time consuming to create and taking the *mean* score tends to hide extreme attitudes.

Likert Scale (1932)

This, the most frequently used measure of attitudes, also consists of statements. However, respondents are able to show *how much* they agree or disagree with them. The statements we have just used would look like the example in Figure 1.10.

Please indicate the extent to which you agree with the statement by circling the response which is closest to your view

1   Aggression adds to the excitement of sport:

   strongly agree / agree / undecided / disagree / strongly disagree

2   Referees should be tougher on aggressive behaviour:

   strongly agree / agree / undecided / disagree / strongly disagree

FIGURE 1.10 *An example of a Likert Scale*

Half the statements should be favourable and half unfavourable, as in Figure 1.10. Statements would be scored from 5 to 1, with favourable statements scoring 5 for 'strongly agree' through to 1 for 'strongly disagree'. Unfavourable statements are scored in the reverse way, with 1 for 'strongly agree' through to 5 for 'strongly disagree'. The scores for each statement are added together to give the individual's attitude score.

Before measuring attitudes using the Likert Scale, researchers would do a pilot study, in order to check that the statements:

■ **are clear**: so respondents will understand what is being said;
■ **are unambiguous**: so that the statements cannot be taken to have two meanings;

■ **distinguish between attitudes**: if everyone answers that they 'strongly agree' with a statement then the statement is not useful in separating people with positive and those with negative attitudes.

Statements which fail these tests are rejected in the final scale. The Likert Scale is easier, faster and cheaper to construct than the Thurstone Scale, and tests show that it is as reliable. However, there is a problem with the middle classification which scores 3: does 3 mean the individual has mixed feelings and is 'undecided' or that he or she is 'neutral'? There is no way of differentiating between these two.

Osgood's Semantic Differential Scales (Osgood, Suci and Tannenbaum, 1957)

These scales were designed to measure what a particular object, issue or experience means to an individual. This is done by providing a list of two opposite words (such as good/bad). Between each pair of words is a seven-point scale and the respondent has to mark the point on the scale which agrees with his or her attitude – the midpoint representing neutral.

Osgood claimed that there were three factors which should be measured through the word-pair items: the evaluative, the activity and the potency factor. A Semantic Differential Scale for aggression in sport might look like the example in Figure 1.11.

Rate how you feel about aggression in sport by drawing a circle round the point which best describes your feelings:

good	+3	+2	+1	0	−1	−2	−3	bad
relaxed	+3	+2	+1	0	−1	−2	−3	tense
beneficial	+3	+2	+1	0	−1	−2	−3	harmful

FIGURE 1.11 *An example of an extract from a Semantic Differential Scale*

This type of scale is simple, fast and direct. However, the word pairs may not have much meaning for the respondent and different respondents may interpret them differently. As noted with the Likert Scale, a midpoint response does not differentiate between neutral and undecided.

Evaluation of attitude scales

Although attitude scales are widely used in research, they need to be constructed with care and the results should be used with caution, because:

- attitudes may be difficult to express in words;
- statements may mean different things to different people;
- the words used in a statement can influence the way people respond;
- people may not be truthful in their responses;
- people tend to agree more than to disagree with statements;
- attitudes are not very good indicators of behaviour;
- attitude scales must show reliability, which means they should produce the same responses when completed again by the same person;
- attitude scales must show validity, which means they should measure what they are supposed to be measuring.

Changing attitudes

We should be able to change behaviour by changing attitudes, but how do attitudes change? Let us look now at three explanations offered by psychologists.

Cognitive dissonance theory

If we return to the player who does not attend warm-ups, he wants to play rugby and knows warm-ups will improve his game and fitness but he does not do them. How does he manage to hold two contradictory ideas? He does so by changing his attitude to one of them, so that there is less contradiction (or dissonance). For instance, he could justify his non-attendance by telling himself that he jogs to the training session so he does not need to do the warm-ups.

Essentially our player is trying to create a balance in his attitudes, to make them consistent. Festinger (1957) explained this in his cognitive dissonance theory. He proposed that we know certain things (have cognitions) about our beliefs, thoughts and attitudes and how they relate to our behaviour. When these cognitions are *inconsistent*, we feel psychological discomfort, which is unpleasant. We try to reduce this feeling of discomfort by changing our cognition. For example we:

- **make it less important** ('Warm-ups don't make much difference to my game');
- **change it** ('Warm-ups can actually create injury');
- **replace it** ('Jogging is just as good').

There has been limited research on attitude change in sport, but one study of cognitive dissonance by Al-Talib (1970) had students play a role which was either consistent with or inconsistent with their attitudes to physical education. His results showed that:

- students who had a positive attitude to PE but who played a role which was *negative* to PE subsequently changed their attitude: it became more negative;
- students with a positive attitude to PE and who played a positive role subsequently showed an even *more* positive attitude.

This study suggests that cognitive dissonance can affect attitudes, as well as highlighting the importance of the coach or teacher in the changing of these attitudes. Coaches and teachers can try to use some of the principles behind cognitive dissonance, for example:

- by emphasising the dissonance: 'If you *really* want to achieve that time by the end of the season then you will have to put in more training'
- by changing the *behaviour*: 'Come on, just have a go for a few minutes' – by trying to make the experience fun and rewarding, a teacher may change a negative attitude to a positive one.

Persuasive communication

Psychologists investigating persuasive communication have often looked at how advertisers can make their messages more persuasive. Hovland, Janis and Kelley (1953) proposed that we need to consider the following factors:

- **the source of the message**: for example, is the person giving the message trustworthy, believable, high status?
- **the message**: for example, is it clear or hidden, presented simply or as an argument, presented verbally or as a picture?
- **the recipients**: for example, how resistant are they, how persuadable, how educated, how important to them are the attitudes they hold?
- **the situation or context**: for example, how formal or informal is it?

For our attitude to change, it appears that we must be receptive to some extent, because, for example, trying to change attitudes by creating fear can work in the opposite direction – making us *more* resistant to change. If the source of the message is a popular sporting figure, then those whose attitudes are not very strongly held, or whose attitudes are not that important to them, may be persuaded to change. For example, this is why we see the 'big names' in sports, such as Gary Lineker, advertising products from crisps to sports shoes. Finally, there should be a good match between the four factors above, for example the style of the message should match the level of education or experience of the recipient – particularly important when trying to change children's attitudes. If these factors are taken into account, it may be possible to change negative attitudes to positive ones.

CHAPTER SUMMARY

This chapter has presented some of the explanations which psychologists have proposed for our behaviour in a sports setting. We have seen that the reasons we take part in sport include the desire to achieve, to be competent, to gain rewards and to win. Nevertheless, we can be deterred by fear of failure or of injury or because we feel controlled. This chapter has identified ways in which we differ as individuals, so we are more likely to persist if the situation we are in matches our individual needs, personality and attitudes. Although there are techniques for measuring some of these characteristics, we have noted that there are weaknesses in these methods, so they must be used with caution.

chapter two

ANALYSING AND PERFORMING SKILLS

CHAPTER OVERVIEW

When Olga Korbut received a perfect score for her routine in the 1972 Olympics, spectators marvelled at her skills. How does such skilled performance come about? Although elite athletes and their coaches are concerned about producing the best possible performance of skills, the learning and control of motor skills are frequently taken for granted by sports participants. Professionals in the fields of physiology, bio-mechanics and psychology have all contributed to a greater understanding of the nature of skilled performance.

One approach in psychology is to study how we take in and store information – known as the information-processing approach. This approach has been used to help us analyse how skills are performed, how they are learned and how the novice differs from the expert. We start this chapter by looking at skills and how they can be classified, before we look at the key features of the information processing approach to skill learning and performance. In Chapter 3, we go on to examine other explanations for how we learn skills.

WHAT IS A SKILL?

Although defining a skill is difficult, it is widely accepted that a skill is *learned*; it can be improved through practice. Knapp (1963) defined skill as:

'the learned ability to bring about pre-determined results with maximum certainty, often with the minimum outlay of time or energy or both.', (p. 4)

This definition captures the key features of a skill, namely that it involves:

■ behaviour that is intended to achieve a specific objective, for example to shoot a basket;
■ gaining maximum results with minimum (intentional) effort (not just through luck) such as to shoot a basket nine times out of ten;

FIGURE 2.1 *Olga Korbut performing in the 1972 Olympics*

- practice before it can be acquired;
- a high quality of performance, related perhaps to the degree of success or the aesthetic quality, for example in ice-dancing and gymnastics.

Whether driving a car, dialling a phone number or shooting a basket, we receive, process and use information and, as a result, are able to perform appropriate movements. To do this we use three different types of skills, these are:

- **perceptual skills**: those used to make sense of information coming to the brain via the senses;
- **cognitive skills**: those relating to thinking, decision-making, planning;
- **motor skills**: those involved in making movements.

In other words, skills involve the combination of perception, cognition and action. Another definition of skill, which recognises these skills and their interaction, is offered by Whiting. He defines skill as:

'complex, intentional actions involving a whole chain of sensory, central and motor mechanisms which through the process of learning have come to be organised and co-ordinated in such a way as to achieve predetermined objectives with maximum certainty.' (Whiting, 1975, p. 6)

The importance of all three skills is reflected in the terms *perceptual–motor skills* or *psychomotor skills*. You may see these shortened to motor skills, but it is important to remember that the term motor skills implies perceptual skills as well. Before we go on to examine these skills in more detail, we will look briefly at the difference between ability and skill, and between different types of skills.

WHAT IS THE DIFFERENCE BETWEEN ABILITY AND SKILL?

Whereas a skill is learned, ability is largely *innate*; it is a general characteristic of the performer which can be used in a variety of skills. Without ability a skill cannot be developed to a high level, for example a child with limited flexibility is unlikely to make a good gymnast. This refers to her motor ability. However, if she can perceive movement very rapidly (a perceptual ability), then she may make a good table-tennis player. This example demonstrates an important aspect of ability: we differ in the degree to which we have particular abilities and this innate difference affects our potential. If this youngster were to take up table-tennis, she would develop her perceptual skills through use and practice. Thus ability is not *learned* (as a skill is learned), it is innate but can be developed through experience.

Researchers such as Fleishman (1964) have tried to identify and classify abilities. He distinguished between two types: gross motor abilities and psychomotor abilities. Let us compare them briefly.

Gross motor abilities

These are seen as general abilities which may be applicable to a number of athletic or physical fitness skills. They refer to speed, strength, co-ordination and flexibility and a selection is listed below.

- **dynamic strength**: muscular endurance in exerting force repeatedly, such as weightlifting;
- **explosive strength**: bursts of muscular effort, as in the long jump;
- **stamina**: capacity to sustain maximum effort requiring cardiovascular effort, as in marathon running;
- **gross body co-ordination**: co-ordination of the action of several parts of the body while it is in motion, as when bowling a cricket ball.

Psychomotor abilities

These abilities more directly involve perceptual abilities, for example:

- **reaction time**: responding rapidly to a stimulus when it occurs, such as the sound of the starting pistol;
- **manual dexterity**: making skilful well-directed arm/hand movements when manipulating objects under speed conditions, as in basketball;
- **aiming**: the ability to aim precisely at a small object in space, as in archery.

Thus, we can see that our abilities underpin skills, and most skills require the use of both types of ability, various abilities being of more or less value in particular skills. Coaches and teachers need to be sensitive to the abilities of learners when practising skills, and, particularly with primary age school children, to provide opportunities for developing these abilities which will form the basis for specific skills later on.

WAYS OF CLASSIFYING SKILLS

Given the range of perceptual–motor skills required in sporting activities, researchers have tended to classify them in several ways. Each of these ways is like a scale (called a continuum) and the skill can be placed in the middle or at either end of the continuum. We will look at six classifications and then use them to analyse two skills – the long jump and dribbling in soccer (see Figure 2.3, p. 38).

Continuous–serial–discrete continuum

Continuous skills have no clear beginning or end (as in cycling), whereas discrete skills (such as a dive) have a beginning and an end which are obvious. Continuous skills can be continued for as long as the performer wishes since the end of one cycle of the skill automatically becomes the beginning of the next. Some skills would be placed in the middle of this continuum and are called serial skills because they do have a beginning and an end but they are repeated in a particular order, for example hurdling.

Part–whole continuum

This refers to the extent to which a skill can be broken down into parts and thus relates to the best method of learning a skill. For instance, hurdling involves a sequence of skills which can be broken down. The athlete can practise clearing the hurdles as a separate element from practising her stride.

Hurdling would be placed towards the *part* end of the continuum. In contrast, a tennis serve involves a number of skills which must be combined and performed at the same time: stance, ball toss, back swing and so on are performed as one whole skill. This point is discussed further under methods of practice in Chapter 3, Learning and Teaching Skills p. 76).

Self–external pacing continuum

This refers to the degree of control which the sportsperson has over the start and timing of an action. The continuum ranges from self-pacing to external pacing. A golfing shot is a self-paced skill because the golfer can decide when to start the shot and how rapidly to perform it. In contrast, when a tennis player returns a serve this is an externally-paced skill because he cannot make his return until the ball comes to him. In addition, the speed with which he performs his return is affected by the speed of the approaching ball and the movement of his opponent (another external factor).

Open–closed continuum

This classification refers to the extent to which environmental conditions affect the performance. Closed skills are performed in a stable and predictable environment, so the performer knows in advance what to do and when to do it (such as a gymnast). Learning closed skills involves refining the skill until it is as perfect as possible and then repeating it until it can be performed automatically (until it is habitual). A gymnast starting a routine is performing a closed skill which is self-paced (see previous classification).

However, closed skills may also occur in an 'open' situation. The netball player taking a penalty shot is performing a closed skill, but she must take account of environmental factors such as the position of other players and likely rebounds. In other words, this penalty shot cannot be purely habitual, it has some of the characteristics of an open skill.

Open skills are those which occur in a constantly changing environment in which the player does not know what will happen and has to make rapid decisions about what to do and when to do it. The basketball player in Figure 2.2 has to be able to control the ball whilst noting the movement of team-mates and opposing players as well as making tactical decisions. Dribbling a basketball is therefore an open skill, which is best learned by practising it under a wide variety of conditions so that it can be performed effectively whatever the circumstances.

FIGURE 2.2 *An excellent example of an open skill*

Gross–fine continuum

Gross skills are those which require the use of major muscles, such as running or jumping; fine skills are those requiring precise movements, using small muscle groups such as those a bowler uses to spin a cricket ball. However, the bowler uses both gross and fine skills in his run-up and delivery, so bowling in cricket would therefore be placed on the middle of the continuum. The use of both types of skill in sports performance is very common.

Intrinsic feedback continuum

This refers to the amount of feedback that the athlete experiences as the skill is performed (for more on feedback, see p. 51.) For example, an athlete in the 200 m will receive considerable feedback from her muscles and from what she sees whilst she is running, but very little as she leaves the starting blocks. A rugby player receives feedback from his pass as he sees the flight of the ball.

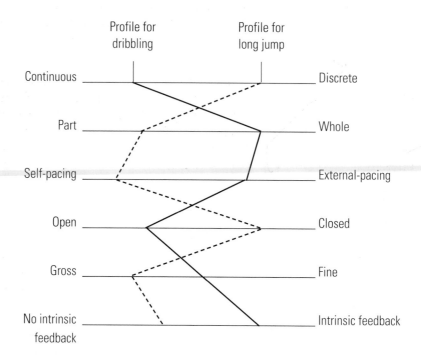

FIGURE 2.3 *Skill profiles for the long jump and dribbling (soccer)*

It is vital that performers and coaches recognise where skills lie on these continua because their position indicates the most effective practice. For details on practices and training see Chapter 3, Learning and Teaching Skills, p. 75.

ANALYSING THE PERFORMANCE OF SKILLS: THE INFORMATION-PROCESSING APPROACH

Having looked at different types of skills, we will now examine the various processes involved when a sportsperson performs a skill. We will see that the type of skill performed (according to Figure 2.3) requires different processes. For example, as we saw on the open–closed continuum, the basketball player has to respond rapidly to a huge variety of input, whereas the gymnast does not need to do this. Performing a skill requires remembering aspects of previous performance such as how the body feels, deciding at what time to commence a movement and how to adjust performance to take account of different circumstances. All of these very complex processes, and the way they work together, can be analysed using the information-processing approach.

This approach views humans as processors of information. For example, a batsman preparing to hit a cricket ball takes in visual information – identifying the ball in the bowler's hand, registering its changing size as it gets closer. This visual information is processed so that the batsman is able to judge the speed of the ball. He must step into the stroke at the right moment with the bat at the correct angle. These movements depend on the decisions he makes about how the ball will bounce and at what speed.

The batsman must also decide how fast to swing the bat to make the stroke he wants to make, so he uses memory of previous experiences to help him make these decisions. After the stroke is made he can 'feel' how good it was. He can also see how good it was by the effect on the ball – did he hit a boundary or did the ball clip the bat and just miss the wicket-keepers' outstretched gloves? This information is also processed and becomes feedback which is stored in memory.

Now let us try to fit all of these activities into an information-processing framework. The incoming information that our batsman received (input)

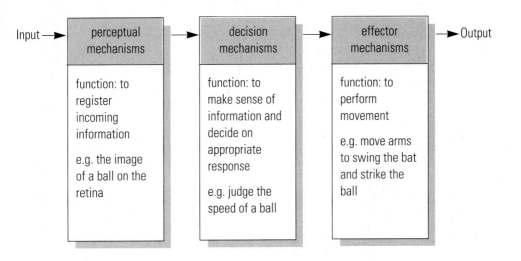

FIGURE 2.4 *The components of perceptual-motor skill performance and their functions (adapted from* Whiting, 1975, p. 10)

was processed through a number of stages before he struck the ball (output). Whiting (1975) clarified this process by first identifying the physical parts involved in the performance of perceptual–motor skills. Figure 2.4 shows these parts and the functions they perform.

Psycholgists have offered a number of explanations and descriptions of what these mechanisms involve, for example Whiting (1975) proposed that they carry out three major functions, namely:

1 **perception**: to make sense of incoming information ('The ball has just left the bowler's hand');
2 **translation**: to decide what is happening and what to do about it ('It's going to bounce short so I'll hook it');
3 **effector control**: to put a motor programme into effect ('Weight on the back foot and play the hook').

Despite considerable research, there is still much that psychologists do not understand about the processes which underlie our ability to perform and learn motor skills. A major difficulty is that they can only infer the mechanisms involved by observing the behaviour; the underlying mechanisms cannot be observed directly. Indeed, the term mechanisms is only one of a number of terms used in the description of human information processing.

For our purposes we will use a simplified diagram (Figure 2.5) which shows an expanded version of Figure 2.4, incorporating the key features of human information-processing and showing how they are thought to be related.

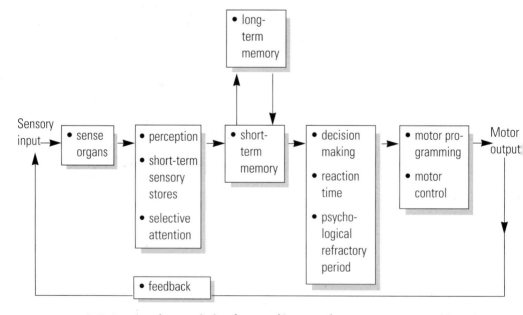

FIGURE 2.5 *Diagram showing the key features of human information-processing and how they are related*

We are now in a position to analyse how a skill is performed by looking at each of the stages shown in Figure 2.5 in more detail.

Sense organs

We take in information from our environment through receptors in our sense organs, which enable us to see, hear, smell, touch and so on. Let us look briefly at the three most important senses for physical activity.

Vision

The eyes take in light waves which are converted into electrical impulses and transmitted to the brain, which then makes sense of them through the process of visual perception (see p. 42). Vision provides us with information about movement of objects in the environment (the position of the cricket ball in flight) and about our position in the environment. Vision appears to be the most important of the senses, as it is estimated that over 90 per cent of the sensory information we receive is taken in through the eyes.

Audition

The ears take in sound waves which are changed to electrical impulses and transmitted to the brain, which then makes sense of what is heard through the process of auditory perception. This enables us to notice and identify aspects of our environment even when we cannot see them, such as hearing a team-mate call from behind us. It also provides information about our own activities – a skilled badminton player can use the sound of the racket strings striking the shuttlecock to judge the quality of a stroke.

Proprioception

The movement of our body in space, its balance, position of limbs and so on, is called proprioceptive information. This information comes from within the body. It is carried by nerve receptors (called proprioceptors) in the muscles, tendons, joints and inner ear. There are three parts to proprioceptive information:

- the sense of **touch** enables us to feel, for example pressure (our grip on a racket);
- the sense of **equilibrium** tells us how balanced we are or the position of our bodies in space: the information comes from sense organs in the inner ear and is of particular importance, for example, to gymnasts and divers;
- **kinaesthesis** is the sense which tells the brain about the movement of muscles, tendons and joints, for example when breaking in a pair of new trainers your feet may feel 'wrong' for a while.

As you can see, each of these senses provides us with feedback about the movements we make. This sensory feedback is generated by the movement itself and is called intrinsic feedback. It enables us to adjust and control movement, and becomes input into the information processing system (see Figure 2.5 and p. 51 later in this chapter).

Perception

Perception is the process by which the brain interprets and makes sense of the information transmitted by the sense organs. It involves several cognitive processes.

Short-term sensory stores

This sensory input is stored very briefly in the short-term sensory stores. There is one for vision and one for audition, so what we see is held in the visual store, what we hear is held in the auditory store. There is also a haptic sensory store for touch, though evidence for a proprioceptive information store is less clear. These sensory memories fade rapidly, within one second, unless they are transmitted to short-term memory for further processing. So, briefly, the batsman will have an image of the ball leaving the bowler's hand, or the sprinter will 'hold' the sound of the starting pistol. Whether or not this information is passed to short-term memory depends on the process of selective attention.

Selective attention

There is a vast amount of sensory information coming into the brain at any one time. Consider the visual information the batsman receives: he sees the ball, the bowler's body, patches of green, some fielders, an umpire, advertising hoardings, spectators, buildings, the sky. This whole picture is called the display. The process of picking out and focussing on the most relevant part of the display is called selective attention (Figure 2.6). Selective attention filters out unnecessary information and allows us to attend only to what is necessary.

It is necessary for information to be selected because the central nervous system does not have the capacity to process all aspects of the environment, so information which is not relevant must be filtered out. Before we look at how this occurs, it is worth noting that this point about capacity is a key point in the information-processing approach. For example, it seems that the more processing capacity we use for one task, the less is available for another. If you are talking yourself through a tennis serve you may hear your coach's voice but will probably be unable to attend to what she is saying sufficiently well to reproduce it. Your processing capacity is almost totally used up in the performance of your serve.

FIGURE 2.6 *This batsman has been able to select information about the flight of the ball from the rich display of visual information he receives*

Kahneman's (1973) theory of attention proposed that there is a limit to our capacity, so, for example, when we are aroused we have greater capacity than when we are tired. If we are skilled at a task, it requires fewer attentional resources than if we are first learning how to do it. Thus, in Kahneman's view, attention is more than a selection process, it is our *capacity* to process information. We will return to the issue of capacity at various points in this information-processing section.

Attention to a particular aspect of a stimulus therefore reduces the load on the information-processing system and prevents the information in the sensory memory store from fading or decaying. However, the information to which our batsman is *not* attending (such as the advertising hoardings) fades rapidly. By the process of selective attention the information is saved for further processing.

Factors which help us select particular information include:

- **expectation**: we tend to look for what we expect, so the skilled batsman pays attention to the bowler's arm action in order to predict delivery of the ball; the learner expects important information when he hears a teacher say 'So the main thing to remember is...';
- **relevance**: we notice that which is relevant to us, such as the bowler's arm action but not a passing aeroplane;

■ **vividness**: we will attend to something which is vivid in contrast to other information, so we notice a sudden move by our opponent, or the words a coach stresses in her instructions.

Just as selective attention can be enhanced by these factors, it can be damaged by over-arousal. This is discussed in Chapter 4, Arousal, Anxiety and Stress in Performance and in Chapter 6 (p. 160) we look at how attention is related to performance.

There are a variety of theories about where selection takes place. For example, Welford (1952) proposed that it occurs at the short-term sensory storage stage, and that the information selected is processed through all the later stages to output (in series). However, others argued that several stimuli can be processed at the same time (in parallel) until filtering occurs during processing in short-term memory. An illustration of information being processed in parallel is the hockey player dribbling the ball down the field, who is able to process information about the relationship between the ball and the stick (visual), the condition of the ground, her balance, her grip on the stick (proprioceptive) and the shouts of her team-mates about their positions (auditory information).

In order to select information, we need to use both short-term and long-term memory, which we will look at now.

Memory

One way of understanding memory is to see it as two stores or stages: incoming information goes first into short-term and then, depending on what happens to it, transfers to long-term memory. We will look at what is known about these stages before we consider how they are related.

Short-term memory

Coaches are advised to 'keep it short' when giving instructions to a learner. This is because short-term memory has a limited capacity (about seven items) and information lasts only a short time (approximately 15–30 seconds) before it fades. Short-term memory can be considered a 'bottle-neck' which prevents some information being transferred to long-term memory.

Because of its limited capacity and short storage time, interference can cause difficulties. This occurs when information already in short-term memory is affected by the entry of new information. When a tennis player is learning to serve, time should be allowed after each serve to let her register the 'feel' of the serve. If time is not allowed – perhaps the player is asked to hit all the balls back to the other end of the court – the 'feel' of the serve (the proprioceptive information) may become confused and the memory lost.

If information continues to be processed (rehearsed) in short-term memory, then it is more likely to be retained and transferred to long-term memory; otherwise it is lost (forgotten).

Long-term memory

Long-term memory is distinguished from short-term memory because it is thought to be able to store a potentially limitless amount of information, and the information can be stored for long periods – months and even years rather than seconds. Skills such as walking and talking, once learned, are usually permanent. Indeed, in comparison with memories of experiences or events, motor skills are fairly resistant to forgetting. For example, the memory for how to swim or cycle does not seem to deteriorate at all. It appears that this may be because the memory for motor skills is stored in part in the muscles and tendons (see Motor control, p. 55), whereas memory for word meanings, for example, is stored exclusively in the brain. The main difficulty in long-term memory is retrieving the information which we have stored there.

The relationship between short-term and long-term memory

Both short-term and long-term memory are involved in perception and decision making. For example, the batsman knows from previous experience that he must focus on the ball as it leaves the bowler's hand. In addition, his experience enables him to select the bowler's arm action from the display, to predict the likely flight of the ball, to refer to his stored knowledge of how such a delivery will bounce on this particular type of pitch, and to prepare to make the appropriate stroke, the memory for which is also stored in long-term memory.

In brief, he is constantly moving to and fro between new information and old information in order to perform the correct stroke. Thus, the information acquired through past experiences (stored in long-term memory) is selected and brought into short-term memory and the new information is compared with it. This is why short-term memory has also been called *working memory* (Baddeley, 1986). Baddeley sees working memory as a system controlled by a central executive, which is able to direct attention to a number of tasks simultaneously, such as making sense of incoming information, deciding what to do about it and planning responses. Clearly, Baddeley sees working memory as far more complex than a simple short-term store: it is related to Kahneman's theory of attention which we referred to earlier (p. 43). We can see that two reasons why the experienced athlete is more effective than the novice is due to the speed with which he can process information and the capacity he has to deal with it.

How can we improve memory?

There are a number of ways in which we can improve memory. Listed below are some of those which are useful in a sports setting.

- **rehearsal**: if we repeat something, we are more likely to remember it. For example, you may repeat a telephone number to yourself until you are able to dial it, or you may practise a netball shot until you can remember the feel of it. This is called rehearsal and helps the memory to last longer, possibly to become fairly permanent.
- **avoid interference**: allow time for new information to 'sink in' and avoid presenting two very similar pieces of information one after the other or they may become confused. For more on this, see Transfer of learning in Chapter 3, Learning and Teaching Skills, p. 71.
- **association**: if new information can be linked to old information (information already stored in long-term memory), then it will be remembered better. The netball teacher might say 'Remember last week when we practised a one/two landing then throwing? This week we'll learn something extra: how to land and change direction before throwing – using the pivot'. Doing this makes new information more meaningful because it becomes associated with information which is already stored.

FIGURE 2.7 *It is easier for a novice to remember new skills if they are linked to skills already learned*

- **organisation**: information is more likely to be remembered if it can be organised in a meaningful way. Research shows that we can remember more words from a list if we organise them by meaning; equally, we can remember motor skills if they are organised. For example, to help the gymnast remember longer and more complex sequences, he should practise putting moves together so that the memory for the end of one move is linked to the memory for the beginning of the next. This organises the sequence in his memory, and relates to the chaining method of practice (for more details see p. 76).
- **chunking**: sometimes information cannot be organised easily, but if it can be chunked together, more of it can be handled at one time. Experience in match play helps a player see her own position in relation to other players more clearly – to see the whole field of play. Information about various patterns of play has become 'chunked' into a larger picture.
- **imagery**: information can be retained better by creating a 'mind picture'. Demonstration of a skill enables the observer to see an image which can be retained in the mind, for example. Information which can be translated into an image, such as a sprinter 'exploding' off the starting blocks, or visualising your limbs as cooked spaghetti when trying to relax, can be an effective way of helping performers remember verbal instructions.

Decision making and reaction times

If we return to our batsman, he has now interpreted the incoming information so his next step is to decide what to do. One way of studying decision making is to measure the time between seeing a stimulus and responding to it, which is known as the reaction time (or RT). Research on reaction time revealed that when participants were shown an array of lights and asked to respond when one was switched on, those who were asked to point to it reacted much faster than those who had to *say* which light it was. This suggests that the decision-making processes involved in pointing are different from those for speaking. It is important to note that:

- **reaction time** is the time between the presentation of a stimulus and the start of a response;
- **movement time** is the time taken to complete a movement after it has been started (this is related to motor programmes, which are covered later in this chapter);
- **response time** is the reaction time *plus* the movement time.

The study of reaction time is important in sports because many activities depend for their success on fast reactions, whether reacting to the starting pistol or responding to an opponent's 'dummy' in volleyball. Researchers have identified several factors that can either increase or decrease reaction time. We will review some now.

Factors affecting reaction time

Stimulus–response compatibility
This refers to the degree to which the stimulus and the response are 'naturally' associated. For example, if the stimulus (such as the sound of a buzzer) comes from the right, response is faster with the right hand than with the left.

Automaticity
The more often a stimulus is responded to, the more reaction time is reduced. For example, the more practice a goalkeeper has in saving shots, the faster his or her reaction time. Eventually the response will become automatic, and it therefore requires virtually no attentional effort.

Anticipation
Reaction time also decreases as the individual learns more about the context in which the events occur. This enables them to anticipate a stimulus, to be prepared and thus to react more speedily. Bakker, Whiting and van der Brug (1990) illustrate this in their quote from Muhammad Ali when he was in difficulties due to his opponent's dangerous left cross. However, Ali explained that, after a while:

> 'I had his movements so catalogued and timed that I knew the meaning of the slight twitch that would involuntarily appear in his throat when he was about to smash the bomb. Then I would cut over his blow.' (p. 321)

This quotation also shows the benefits of *attention* and *automaticity* – practising until performance becomes automatic. Because he was so well practised, Muhammad Ali was able to attend to crucial aspects of his environment that he might otherwise have overlooked if his attention had been directed at his own performance.

The number of stimuli
Hick (1952) found that as the number of stimuli increased, the reaction time increased by a consistent amount. He proposed *Hick's Law* which states that reaction time is related to the amount of information that must be processed in order to respond. In other words, the more choices we have to make, the longer it takes to react. It is useful, therefore, to distinguish between:

- **simple reaction time** (SRT) – where there is one stimulus and the athlete is expecting it (for example the starting pistol);
- **choice reaction time** (CRT) – where there are several stimuli and the athlete has to choose which one to respond to (such as the movements of several players on the basketball court).

This has implications for sportspeople. For example, in a tennis game the greater the variety of shots you can make from one position on the court, the slower your opponent will be in responding to the shot you do make.

However, the amount of information the *novice* has to process may also damage performance because the novice is trying to produce the correct movement as well as respond to a stimulus. This is particularly evident in youngsters, whose ability to attend to information is more limited than that of adults. In open or externally paced skills, there are a variety of stimuli which are likely to slow decision making, so skills required in team games such as soccer or hockey are best practised between two learners, or in a two versus two, or three versus three format.

The timing of stimuli
If we do not have time to complete an action before the next stimulus occurs, it takes us longer to respond to the second stimulus. Welford (1952) proposed that we have a single channel for processing information, which means we have to complete our response to one 'item' of information before we can start to process new information (which is called processing in series, see selective attention p. 44). As we can only process one item of information at a time, our response to later information is likely to be delayed. This happens when, for example, a player makes a 'fake' move to the right and the opponent responds to cover the move. If the player then rapidly pushes off to the left, the opponent will still be moving in the opposite direction. It takes the opponent longer to follow the move to the left than if the other player had only made that move to the left. This additional delay is called the psychological refractory period (PRP). Figure 2.8 shows the PRP in terms of a basketball 'fake'.

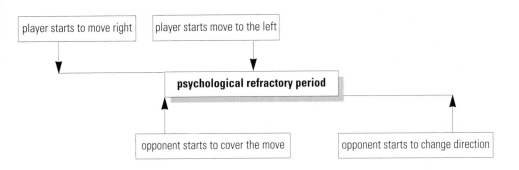

FIGURE 2.8 *Diagram showing psychological refractory period in terms of a basketball 'fake'*

Motor programmes

Once the decision-making stage has been completed and a plan of action chosen, the sportsperson has to organise the necessary commands to the muscles so that the action can be put into effect. The memory for this set of movements is called a motor programme. It is put into effect by the effector mechanism – the nerves and muscles which serve the limbs involved in the movement.

Performance of a motor programme also involves very complex processes: muscle movement must occur in the correct sequence, some information must be sent very rapidly, the necessary movements may not be well learned, inaccurate movement must be adjusted, the plan of action may be uncertain.

A motor programme can be seen as consisting of simple subroutines which can be grouped together to perform a movement. The programme which organises these subroutines is called an *executive* programme. It organises the subroutines into the correct sequence and adapts movement to changes in the environment. Thus, motor skills have a hierarchical structure in which sub-routines are organised by 'higher' programmes. Figure 2.9 illustrates this hierarchy using an overhead clear in badminton as an example.

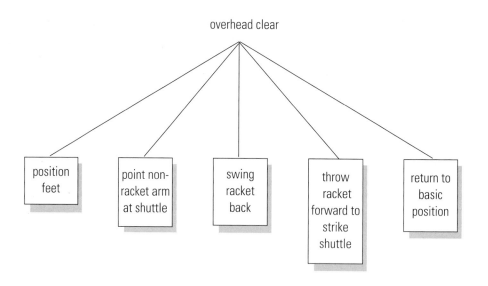

FIGURE 2.9 *The hierarchical structure of an overhead clear for a novice badminton player*

Fitts and Posner (1967) suggest that the lowest of the subroutines are fixed sequences of movements which we perform automatically, because we have previously learned them. These subroutines are learned during the first few years of life, and form the basis for perceptual–motor skills. Subroutines will be combined in different ways to perform different skills. Learning these skills therefore involves organising the subroutines into a new executive programme.

As the performer becomes more skilful, executive programmes become automatic subroutines of larger and more complex executive programmes. For the elite badminton player, the overhead clear will be a subroutine in an executive programme for 'shots to be taken above the head'.

We have already noted that as skills become learned they become automatic, that through practice the executive programme can become a subroutine, but just how does this occur? The next section offers some of the answers, as provided by the information-processing approach.

LEARNING SKILLS: THE INFORMATION-PROCESSING APPROACH

So far, we have stressed the performance of skills, but in order to explain how skills are acquired we need first to look at feedback (see Figure 2.5). We can then move on to examine how we use feedback to control movement (motor control) and to consider theories of motor learning.

Feedback

Feedback occurs as the result of an action. It allows us to compare our performance with the 'model' of the correct skill and thus to note errors and make adjustments. It tells us about the appropriateness or accuracy of the action so that we can monitor and adapt our behaviour as a result of previous performance – in other words, it is involved in the explanation of how we *learn* skills.

Types of feedback

Feedback, like any other incoming information, has to be processed: this can be seen from Figure 2.5 on p. 40. We receive two types of feedback:

■ **intrinsic feedback** occurs as a natural consequence of the movement and is received by the senses (the feel of a headstand or the sound of the ball on the racket);

■ **extrinsic feedback** is external to the performer and is sometimes called extra or supplementary feedback (such as provided by a coach or a video).

Figure 2.10 shows the various types of feedback; each of them provides only partial information about the performance of a psychomotor skill. For example, diving provides only proprioceptive information, whereas the badminton player receives additional intrinsic feedback when he makes a shot (such as hearing a mis-timed shot when the racket frame strikes the shuttle and seeing the shuttle fly out of court).

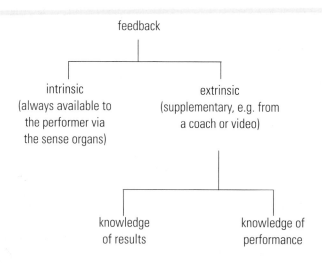

FIGURE 2.10 *Diagram showing the various types of feedback in learning motor skills*

Skills which provide limited intrinsic feedback require extrinsic feedback to supplement the performer's information. For example, the diver depends on her coach for this extra feedback. Extrinsic feedback is particularly useful for beginners as they tend to be less aware of proprioceptive information (such as the position of their limbs) than skilled performers. So extrinsic feedback from the coach ('That follow-through was nice. Can you feel how your arm came through?') helps the learner to recognise and use intrinsic feedback. Extrinsic feedback may be one of two types.

■ **Knowledge of results** (KR) has been used to refer to knowledge about the outcome of an action (such as lap times, distance jumped, number of targets hit). It is knowledge of results that has received the most research because it has been easier to measure.
■ **Knowledge of performance** (KP) relates to information about the perform-ance of the action. The teacher or coach is the key source of this knowledge for the novice or intermediate sportsperson, although team-mates also

play a part. This is one of the benefits of the *reciprocal* (or paired) teaching style in which learners take it in turns to watch the other's performance and provide feedback (see p. 85). Technological developments – such as videos, slow motion replays and computer processing of complex actions by attaching light-emitting diodes (LEDs) to parts of the athlete's limbs – have greatly enhanced knowledge of performance (Figure 2.11). They provide much more detailed information about the movement and co-ordination of limbs, which is particularly valuable to the elite athlete, the coach, and the sports researcher.

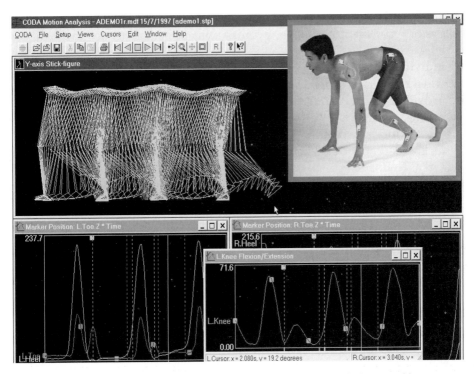

FIGURE 2.11 *Computer imaging produced when LED markers are attached to an athlete in action (inset)*

Characteristics of effective feedback

The coach's role in providing effective feedback is covered in more detail in Chapter 3, Learning and Teaching Skills. Our concern here is to consider how the performer *processes* feedback and therefore which types of feedback are most appropriate and at what stage of the performer's development. Taking a young gymnast learning the backward roll as an example, we will look at some features of effective extrinsic feedback, according to the information-processing approach. Teachers should ensure that feedback is:

- **limited**, because the performer can only process a small amount of information at a time, particularly in the early stages of learning a skill. (This example of feedback will overload the novice: 'No, you fell over because you were too late putting your hand down and you didn't tuck in tight enough. Push harder before you start to open out and try to land on the balls of your feet')
- **focused on specific points** to enable the performer to attend to what is important. ('Hands close to your head and think 'tight' as you push over.')
- **immediate**, occurring as soon as the roll as been performed so that proprioceptive information (the feel of the action) is still strong in the gymnast's memory. If feedback is delayed, subsequent information may distort the original memory, so the gymnast will be unable to use the feedback effectively.
- **individualised**, given to each youngster individually, not the whole group when they have completed their backward rolls.
- **provided using different methods**, such as verbal and visual. (The youngster may not fully understand what a 'tight tuck' means. If the teacher models what the youngster did and then demonstrates the correct tuck and points out where the knees should be, this provides visual and verbal feedback.)
- **aimed at helping the athlete recognise intrinsic feedback**; by learning to register variations in her own body movement, force, balance and so on, the athlete is able to adjust her own performance and perform more skilfully, with less dependence on extrinsic feedback. ('Remember how your knees feel close to your chest'.)

Research on feedback which was conducted by den Brinker (1979) and described by Bakker et al. (1990) illustrates the role of feedback in performance.

RESEARCH
den Brinker (1979)

This research investigated speed skaters participating in competitive selections for the Dutch championships. Half of them received feedback in the form of video recordings of their events, which they then discussed with the trainers. The other half had no such feedback. By the end of the season, the first group had significantly improved their skating technique when compared to those who had received normal training. However, this did not lead to improvement in times, Bakker et al. (1990) note that perhaps the improved techniques must become further automated before times improve.

Motor control

We have already noted that subroutines have to be learned. This occurs when we receive feedback from an action which enables us to change the action when we perform it again. By consciously controlling the action we perform it more accurately. With practice (repeating the action and adapting it as a result of feedback), we need less conscious control, and the movement is performed with greater proficiency.

Marteniuk (1976) noted that because some movements are performed very rapidly, there is no time for feedback to be used to control the movement. He has proposed *levels* of movement control which correspond to the degree to which the performer's central nervous system is involved in control of the movement. Thus, three levels of control can be identified, the differences between them being the role of feedback, the subconscious and the level of attention required. These are shown in Figure 2.12 and explained below.

- **The first level** is automatic and requires no conscious control. The movements happen so quickly that feedback seems unnecessary, for example in skipping. It appears as if, once a decision has been made and a plan of action selected, the motor programme directs the effector system to carry it out. The programme contains all the commands necessary to put it into effect. It is so well learned that it is run off in exactly the same way every time and requires no feedback. Because the control mechanism produces the movement without feedback, this is called open loop control, and it therefore makes no attentional demands on the information-processing system.
- **The second level** involves some feedback which is received by the muscles, thus 'closing' the feedback loop. The muscles then make the necessary adjustments. Marteniuk calls this a reflexive feedback loop, providing feedback between the muscle spindles and muscles in the limbs. This process takes place unconsciously and therefore rapidly, although it does require some attention. An example would be maintaining balance in a headstand.
- **The third level** also involves closed loop control but feedback is through the brain as well as the muscles, because some degree of conscious effort is required to control the skill. It takes time to evaluate the movement consciously and to make adjustments, so control of movements may be poor: movements may be slow, jerky and unco-ordinated. This can be seen when a novice is learning a skill, or when control of a movement has been lost and is being consciously re-established, such as when a gymnast comes off the parallel bars and has to re-start his routine. A similar effect occurs if you think about what each foot is doing when you are skipping.

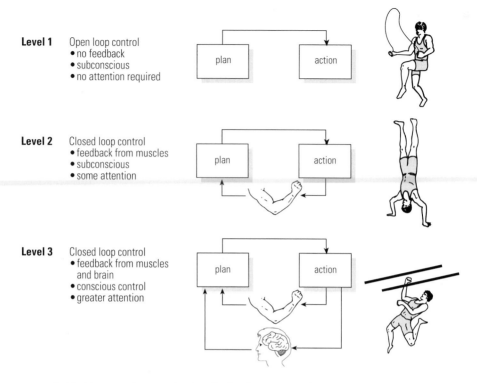

Level 1   Open loop control
             • no feedback
             • subconscious
             • no attention required

Level 2   Closed loop control
             • feedback from muscles
             • subconscious
             • some attention

Level 3   Closed loop control
             • feedback from muscles
               and brain
             • conscious control
             • greater attention

FIGURE 2.12 *Diagram showing the three levels of motor control*

We have established that feedback is necessary in the *learning* of skills, but perhaps not necessary in the performance of some skills; the more automatic the skill, the less feedback is required. This means that the skill *itself* cannot be identified as a first or third level skill; it depends on how well learned it is. So, as we saw on p. 50, an overhead clear in badminton would involve the third level of control when performed by a novice, but the first level of control when performed by an international player.

So far we have talked about what is involved in the control of motor programmes and how they become more automatic, but we have not looked at how we integrate the feedback into current knowledge, and how we remember all this information. Consider what happens when you write your signature. Whether you write it large or small, rapidly or slowly, in felt tip or a fine pen, sitting comfortably or writing in the sand, it always looks recognisably the same. If you sign with your eyes closed, it even looks the same. Is this because you have a motor programme for every one of these circumstances and, depending on the circumstances, the appropriate programme is triggered? This does not account for signing your name in new circumstances. So, is the motor programme for signing your name quite flexible, which enables it to respond to all of these situations yet still produce a consistent outcome? If so, how do we store such a flexible memory?

This concern about flexibility relates to the topic of open skills, which has been noted at several points in this chapter. You will remember that open skills are those performed in ever-changing environments. The performance of the skill must be tailored to a particular set of circumstances which will be different every time the skill is performed. This debate about various types of skills, how they are controlled, the role of feedback and the nature of memory in skill learning has been addressed by a number of psychologists. Let us examine explanations which have been proposed by Adams and by Schmidt.

Theories of motor learning

Adams' Closed Loop Theory

Adams (1971) proposed that motor programmes involve two types of information:

- **the memory trace**, which recalls the appropriate response from memory of previous correct responses, and then initiates the movement. The memory trace does not control movement, it requires no feedback and functions as an open loop system of control.
- **the perceptual trace** controls movement once it is initiated. This trace uses feedback from our limbs, and therefore functions as a closed loop system of control. It compares this feedback with the memory for the correct movement learned previously, and brings the limbs closer to this reference for correctness. The perceptual trace becomes stronger as the movement becomes more accurate.

Schmidt (1975) criticised Adams' Closed Loop Theory because he said it depends on feedback, which is not always used. Adams failed to recognise the role of open loop processes, which are involved in the performance of rapid or automatic responses that are so common in sports activities. In addition, Adams' theory predicts that learning will be most effective the more accurate it is, so *variability* in practice should hinder learning. Research does not support this; in fact, children learn more effectively when they have variable experiences. In addition, Adams' theory suggests memory for a vast number of detailed motor programmes, whereas Schmidt argues that it is more useful to see motor programmes as *generalised* memories for action. His ideas are described below.

Schmidt's Schema Theory

Schmidt formulated his Schema Theory, which includes reference to open loop control and an explanation for how variability in practice can improve motor control. The Schema Theory contends that we acquire skills by learning rules about the functioning of our bodies, forming relationships between how our muscles are activated, what they actually do, how those actions feel,

FIGURE 2.13 *Which theory best explains the way this badminton player learned her skills –*
Adams' or Schmidt's theory?

and memorising this information. We do this through experience, so a
schema is another name for the memory of those relationships. However this
schema is not comprised of all the memories, as Adams implies, but we
extract the central or general features of the memories and it is these which
are stored. Schmidt (1975) argues that after making a movement, the individual
briefly stores four types of information, in the following order.

1 **the initial conditions**, such as the state of the muscles and the environment before movement started, for example in a tennis serve the body
   position, the weight of the tennis ball;
2 **certain aspects of the movement**, which comprise a general motor
   programme for action, such as the amount of back swing, the speed of
   the racket coming through;
3 **knowledge of the results** of the movement, such as where the ball landed
   in the court: Schmidt argues that knowing the outcome of the movement
   is one of the most crucial aspects because it is the outcome of movement
   that enables the strength of the schema to develop;
4 **knowledge of the sensory consequences** of the movement, such as how
   it felt, looked, sounded and so on.

In order to learn a skill successfully, these four types of information must be
present. They are stored only long enough for the performer to abstract some

relationships among them. The relationships are stored in recall memory (which is responsible for the *production* of a movement) and recognition memory (which is responsible for *evaluating* the movement). Thus the memory which produces the action is different from the memory which evaluates its correctness. Let us look at these two types of memory, or schema.

Recall schema

This is responsible for generating a motor programme for an action. It does so using memory of the initial conditions, the aspects of the appropriate motor programme and the knowledge of results (numbers 1–3 above). With each successive performance of the movement the relationship between these three is modified. For example, when learning to serve in badminton, the relationship between the initial position of the racket head and the speed of the shuttle's fall is evaluated and the forward speed of the racket is adjusted to make correct contact with the shuttle. Through repetition and knowledge of results, movements relating to better outcomes are recalled, unsuccessful ones are 'forgotten'. Slowly, a successful relationship emerges: this is the recall schema for a badminton serve.

Recognition schema

This is used to evaluate responses, and Schmidt proposed that it develops using memory for the initial conditions, the knowledge of results and the memory of sensory consequences (numbers 1, 3 and 4 above). Using these three memories, the badminton player can estimate what the movement will feel and sound like – she can estimate (or anticipate) the expected sensory consequences of serving. This is the 'model' against which she will then test the movement (and is similar to Adams' perceptual trace).

THE INFORMATION-PROCESSING APPROACH AND THE COACH

In this chapter we have seen a number of examples of how the coach can use ideas from the information-processing approach to help the learner. As we review the chapter, we can identify some useful pointers.

The three mechanisms of information-processing

In Figure 2.4 (p. 39), we looked at three mechanisms identified by Whiting in the performance of perceptual–motor skills. We can use these when analysing the performance of a skill, for example, a soccer coach who is trying to identify the cause of a player's error might focus on each mechanism in turn:

- **perceptual mechanism**: does the player judge the flight of the ball correctly?
- **decision mechanism**: is he taking too long to decide which shot to play?
- **effector mechanism**: does the shot go over the goal because he kicks underneath the ball?

The key processes

We have examined how the performer transforms incoming information in order to produce appropriate movement. This includes not only incoming information provided by a rapidly approaching cricket ball, but also information provided by teachers or coaches to aid in the development of skills. From the teacher or coach, the learner receives information which he or she has to process: to take in, select for attention, interpret, integrate with previous information and put into effect. Therefore features such as selective attention, the capacity of short-term memory and feedback are applicable to processing *verbal* information just as they are to producing skilled performance.

When providing information, the coach can play a particularly important role in the following processes:

- **selective attention**: to help the performer focus on what is important at that time (see p. 42);
- **memory**: to help the performer remember information by providing links and presenting it in appropriate ways (see p. 44);
- **reaction time**: to increase the speed of reactions by developing anticipation and through practice, and to help players use a 'dummy' or a 'feint' to gain advantage (because of the psychological refractory period, see p. 47)
- **feedback**: to use several types of feedback, ensure it is appropriate, and encourage athletes to recognise and use it (see p. 51).

Practices and the information-processing approach

The purpose of practice is to enable the performer to become more proficient. Ideas generated from the information-processing approach suggest that a coach should break the skill down into its component subroutines, which the learner practises until they are sufficiently established to be linked together into an executive programme. Whether classed as closed or open, a skill requires feedback whilst it is being learned, in order to rectify errors or to link sequences of skills which are being 'chained' together. Once the skill has become automated, it does not require feedback; in other words, this skill is an example of open loop control.

Although closed skills (those performed in a stable, predictable environment such as a dive) are thought to require exact repetition in order to become automated, defining skills as either closed or open is seen as too simplistic. Most skills have both closed and open elements, so variability in the practice of skills is likely to be advantageous. According to Schmidt's Schema Theory, variability in practice provides particular advantages to the learner, namely:

- it enables the learner to respond to a wide variety of stimuli: if a sportsperson's schema for striking a ball is built up from a variety of circumstances (striking a ball in rounders or hockey or squash and under a variety of conditions, at different speeds, different directions, different light conditions), the schema helps the performer become more flexible and so more proficient in novel situations in the future;
- because each individual's abilities and experiences are different, performers register, compare and remember information in their own particular way: variability in practice enables them to learn in this individualised way, rather than the more rigid way provided by, say, drill training (see p. 66).

Stages of skill learning

Effective coaching must be tailored to the performer, taking account of factors such as age, skill level, motivation and ability. We have seen that the information-processing approach recognises the importance of both age and skill level in our processing of information, for example the novice cannot attend to as much information as the expert. These ideas are combined in the stages of skill learning outlined by Fitts and Posner (1967), who proposed that progression from novice to expert has three phases. These phases are described below, and related to the three levels of motor control (see page 55). We can also identify the role of feedback and practice in helping the performer move through each stage.

1 Early or cognitive phase

Behaviour at this stage is, according to Fitts and Posner (1967):

> 'a 'patchwork' of old habits ready to be put together in new patterns, and supplemented by a few new habits.' (p. 12)

The learner selects those 'old habits' (subroutines) which are necessary to perform the skill – putting them together is the beginning of the executive programme for that skill. Thus, the learner's main concern is to understand what he or she has to do and how to attempt the first few trials. It is useful if the coach directs the learner's attention to cues which will aid in the performance of the skill. These will later go unnoticed when the learner is more skilled.

The early stage of skill learning requires considerable cognitive activity, and novices may have difficulties coping with it all. Knowledge is in terms of 'facts' which the novice knows and is trying to perform. A novice badminton player who can just serve over the net may muff his serve when he also starts to think about where to stand after the serve. This is because the novice is holding new information verbally. Our badminton player may be giving himself serving instructions ('wrist cocked, look at the tape') and positioning instructions ('serve high, move back') at the same time. Because this creates considerable demand on his ability to process information and to control his movements, he gets confused and errors occur. This early phase relates to the third level of motor control (see p. 55).

Fitts and Posner note that learners have to learn to know what their limbs are doing, so coaches should direct the learner's attention to the proprioceptive information they receive. Coaches can help learners attend to the relevant cues and give feedback – both knowledge of results and knowledge of performance. During this phase, successful actions are retained and unsuccessful ones discarded, so progress appears to be rapid.

2 Intermediate or associative phase

This phase begins when the learner can perform the action, but starts to learn how to refine it so that it is performed more effectively and consistently. Smoother patterns of movement begin to emerge as the learner is moving towards the second level of motor control. This is the practice phase, so types of practice (see p. 75) are key features during this stage. The performer begins to monitor his or her own feedback, but supplementary feedback needs to be more detailed and exacting than in the first phase.

Anticipation develops, which enables the performer to respond more rapidly, and attention is used more appropriately, so that the performer can successfully respond to a changing environment and perform the skill effectively. As the stage progresses, the improvements in performance become slower and less noticeable; less cognitive and physical effort is required.

3 Final or autonomous phase

After considerable practice, the player enters this phase because skills have become so well learned that they are performed almost automatically. The skills require no feedback, so they are being performed under open loop control (the first level of motor control). During this phase, the player must keep practising, for example drills, to improve the degree of automaticity or to refine style. Thus, the skill is performed with high speed and efficiency.

Improvements in performance are slow, performers must be highly motivated to practise for extensive periods with marginal improvements. This phase requires very little cognitive effort, so the player can concentrate on the best strategy to cope with an opponent's play, or actively block out distracting thoughts and leave the playing of the shots to automatic responses.

CHAPTER SUMMARY

We started the chapter by trying to analyse and classify skills and abilities. Knowing some of their characteristics enables to us understand how they are learned and performed by looking at what mental processes might be involved in different types of skill and at various levels of proficiency. Awareness of these mental processes helps us to recognise what stage of skill learning a performer is at, and therefore to be more effective in our teaching.

chapter three

CHAPTER OVERVIEW

In the previous chapter we looked at different types of skills and how, according to the information-processing view, we learn and perform them. We also noted that because of the difficulty of knowing precisely what is going on in the brain, many of the proposals are very speculative. For some psychologists working earlier this century, the 'black box' of the brain was so unknowable that they studied only what can be known. Essentially this was behaviour which could be observed and whatever caused the behaviour in the first place, known as the stimulus. There are a number of theories which explain learning as making an association between a stimulus and a response; we will look at these first. After considering alternative theories of learning, we move on to look at the relationship between learning and performance, and finally we examine ways in which the teacher or coach can improve performance by making the learning of skills more effective.

ASSOCIATIONIST THEORIES
OF LEARNING

Learning has been defined by Coon (1983) as:

'a relatively permanent change in behaviour due to past experience.'

In this sense, learning does not refer to changes which depend on maturation – such as the change from crawling to walking in babies. Associationist explanations are concerned with the relationship between a stimulus and its response: for example, a youngster who sees his soccer kit (stimulus) and becomes nervous (response) has learned to associate his kit with being in a game situation. This is an example of classical conditioning, the first of the stimulus–response (or S–R) theories.

Classical conditioning

Ivan Pavlov, a Russian physiologist, was studying digestion in dogs in the early 1900s. He noticed that over a period of time the dogs started to produce saliva when they heard the researcher's footsteps approaching. It seemed that the animals learned to associate the footsteps with the food the researcher brought, because they had been presented together so many times.

This is known as *classical conditioning* – when a stimulus which causes an automatic or innate response (as food automatically causes salivation in dogs) becomes associated with an unrelated stimulus (the footsteps). Finally, the new, unrelated stimulus (the footsteps) causes the automatic response.

This sequence of learning is illustrated in Figure 3.1, using our young soccer player as an example. The stimulus which causes the automatic response is called the *unconditional stimulus* (playing in the match) and the stimulus which has become associated with it is called the *conditional stimulus* (the soccer kit). You can see that although nervousness is always the response, it is called the unconditional response when it occurs in the game but the conditional response when it occurs at the sight of the kit.

		Stimulus	Response
1	The situation before conditioning occurs:	playing in a match → (unconditional stimulus)	causes nervousness (unconditional resonse)
		soccer kit →	causes no response
2	The two stimuli are paired together:	boy plays in several → matches wearing soccer kit	causes nervousness
3	When conditioning has occurred:	soccer kit → (conditional stimulus)	causes nervousness (conditional response)

FIGURE 3.1 *The stages in classical conditioning*

Applications of classical conditioning

Classical conditioning can be used to control automatic responses which may damage performance. If performers can learn to relax and associate that relaxation with a particular phrase ('d-e-e-p breath'), they are able to trigger relaxation when they use that phrase. Equally, if performers want to create a state of alertness, they can learn to associate this state with a trigger word such as 'Go!'

This type of association is used when teachers or instructors wish to trigger automatic or habitual responses in their students. An example of its use is in drill training, which was the way in which physical activities were conducted in the early decades of this century. In education, the physical training syllabus in 1919 aimed to accustom the body to 'external suggestions and stimuli'. In drill training, the children stood in rows, facing the teacher, who issued commands, or instructions. Children had to obey in unison, raising their arms or knees, stretching upward, bending the trunk forward, and so on. This is an example of the *command* style of teaching (see p. 84) and may still be appropriate for a particular purpose or for the development of simple movements.

However, classical conditioning and drill training do not help us to learn complex skills, so we need to look at the stimulus–response association in another way in order to do that.

Thorndike's laws of learning

From his work on 'trial and error' learning, Edward Thorndike (1931) proposed a number of laws of learning which explained how the association or bond between a stimulus and response is learned. These explain how new behaviour occurs, for example how a youngster learns to shoot a basket. The three most important laws are the:

- **Law of Readiness**: the individual must be physically and psychologically able to perform the action – the youngster must be strong enough to hold and throw a basketball and must want to do it.
- **Law of Effect**: the development of the stimulus–response bond depends on the consequences the behaviour has for the individual. If the consequences of an action are pleasant, the bond will be strengthened; if they are unpleasant, the bond will be weakened. If the youngster tries and sometimes hits the hoop or if someone says 'Good try' or 'Nearly had it', these are pleasant consequences so he is likely to keep on trying. If he fails continually or someone tells him 'You're no good', then the bond will be weakened and he will probably stop trying.
- **Law of Exercise**: the bond between the stimulus and the response will be strengthened if there is regular and correct practice – the youngster will need to practise shooting a basket.

Operant conditioning

These ideas were developed further by B.F. Skinner, who noted that it is the effect of our voluntary (as opposed to automatic) actions which determines whether or not we repeat them: he said 'behaviour is shaped and maintained by its consequences'. As we 'operate' on our environment, he argued that:

- *pleasant* consequences will *strengthen* behaviour, through the process of either *positive* or *negative* reinforcement;
- *unpleasant* consequences will *weaken* behaviour, through the process of *punish*ment.

By applying these principles, we should be able to improve a sportsperson's performance and reduce the number of errors. In addition, we can affect motivation, team spirit and a myriad of other elements which contribute to high levels of participation and performance. We will now look at the principles of reinforcement and punishment together with some ideas of how they can be applied in a sports setting.

Positive reinforcement

A young hockey player makes an accurate pass and her teacher shouts 'Nice one Lisa'; the youngster grins with delight. Lisa's behaviour (the accurate pass) has brought pleasant consequences (approval from her teacher), so Lisa is more likely to try to make an accurate pass next time. If the teacher waits until half-time to say 'Nice one', this reinforcement will probably not be as effective. The sooner after the action that the reinforcement is given, the more likely it is to be repeated. To be effective in strengthening behaviour, the consequence of an action must be rewarding to the individual, For example, public praise may be pleasant for one performer but embarrassing for another.

Negative reinforcement

Behaviour can also be strengthened (reinforced) if the consequences bring relief from something that is unpleasant. A child who does not enjoy physical activity will find the PE sessions in school unpleasant, he tries his best but becomes increasingly miserable at his ineptitude. Finally he makes no effort to vault onto the box and the teacher tells him to go and do a simple balancing task instead. He has learned that the consequences of 'not trying' are pleasant – he gets let off the difficult work. Thus, he is likely to 'not try' in the future – this behaviour has been strengthened.

Variable schedule of reinforcement

Too much reinforcement may be damaging. When we want the learner to gain a skill, it is valuable to provide reinforcement in the early stages, but this should be reduced fairly quickly so that it is only intermittent. Research shows, for example, that if the learner receives continuous reinforcement, he may stop performing if reinforcement stops. However, if reinforcement becomes intermittent (the occasional 'Nice action'), the appropriate behaviour continues for much longer after reinforcement stops.

This is linked to *extrinsic* and *intrinsic* motivation (see p. 7). The point here is that a sportsperson who is mainly motivated by external rewards (such as praise from the coach, winning a medal, approval from supporters) will be less motivated if these rewards are withdrawn. The aim for the coach is to help the learner find his own (internal) rewards. For example, when learning the tennis serve, the novice hears the coach's positive comments and is encouraged to remember how it felt to do it right – he will gain satisfaction from the correct performance of the skill. This satisfaction is intrinsic – it is something he generates for himself. Thus, he becomes a more independent learner.

Punishment

Punishment has the opposite effect on behaviour – it weakens it. If a behaviour brings unpleasant consequences, the individual is less likely to repeat it. So punishment should stop a player from performing an unwanted behaviour, which is the purpose of the yellow card in soccer. Research shows, however, that punishment is not a particularly successful technique – it may create resentment, dislike and anger. A more successful approach to correcting errors or weakening unwanted behaviour is, where possible to:

- reward correct behaviour and ignore incorrect behaviour;
- frame criticism or negative comments in a positive way ('That was a good try but you still need to start your back swing much earlier').

Punishment may not be so apparent, though. Take, for example, a player who has learned volleyball in a social club. She joins a league club and is suddenly surrounded by much more able players and feels that her level of play is spoiling their game. This is unpleasant and she may leave the club. This is why teachers and coaches should try to ensure success when a player is new to a game or skill: to experience failure is unpleasant – it acts as punishment and tends to weaken behaviour.

Drive reduction theory

Hull (1951) used the principle of a bond being created between a stimulus and a response, but he proposed that the bond was created because of *drive*, which creates motivation. In simple terms, he argued that the need to solve a problem (serve the ball in the right court) creates a drive or motivation to satisfy this need. When we solve the problem (the ball goes in court) this reduces the drive, which is reinforcing. Because our success is rewarding we continue, and so drive is reduced even more and learning takes place. Eventually, a 'habit' is developed – successful performance.

This notion of *habit* is important for learning because Hull argues that as a skill becomes a habit, it requires less and less drive, but it is the drive which motivates behaviour and strengthens the skill. There are two important implications in this for the coach:

- the coach needs to supply a new challenge once a skill is well learned in order to maintain the drive. The coach must provide a new 'problem', such as a more complex skill, in order to maintain drive;
- the more a skill is performed or practised, the greater the player's inhibition. This causes a *decrease* in performance not an increase (as operant conditioning would predict). For example, after 50 serves your performance may be worse than it was on the 35th serve, this is because you have built up an inhibition. However, after a break your performance is likely to be much closer to your best previous standard and will then improve until inhibition occurs again. This is an example that shows performance may not be an accurate indicator of learning. We look at types of practice later in this chapter (see p. 77) and it can be seen that massed (or continuous) practice is likely to lead to inhibition and should be used with care.

ALTERNATIVE THEORIES OF LEARNING

Social or observational learning

Psychologists dissatisfied with the simple emphasis on stimulus and response turned their attention to how we learn by just watching other people (called observational learning) and why we seem to pay attention to some people and not to others. Because learning like this is so dependent on the social setting, it is known as social learning theory. The leading figure in this theory is Albert Bandura (1977a), who proposed that we copy, or model, the behaviour of significant others. These are people who are important to us, because they are:

- **similar** to us (in age, sex, attitude, or because they play the same sport, for example);
- **powerful**, influential or high status (such as parents, teachers, coaches, sports heroes);
- **caring** (parents, friends, coaches, team-mates);
- **rewarded** for their behaviour (someone who achieves success, who wins trophies, who is congratulated).

The sportsperson learns and develops skills by observation of these significant others. For example, in the high jump an athlete may notice the way an elite athlete approaches the bar and may try to reproduce it. It is more likely that the athlete will reproduce the behaviour if the elite performer was successful. In order to model behaviour we need to notice it, remember it and be able to reproduce it. This has particular implications for the way in which skills are taught because teachers or coaches frequently model the desired skill (Figure

3.2). We therefore look at observational learning in more detail later in this chapter, under the section Making skill learning more effective, see p. 75.

FIGURE 3.2 *Ryan Giggs modelling ball skills*

Gestalt theory

Gestalt theory says 'the whole is greater than the sum of its parts'. In other words, we should look at how individuals 'put together' their past and present experiences in order to do what they do in any given situation. Therefore, the consequences of their actions (which is a key part of the behaviourist explanation for learning) will be only *part* of their learning. Of greater interest to the Gestalt theorists is the active part which learners play in making sense of their experiences, which give these experiences personal meaning and can lead to insight learning.

Personal meaning

Because of the importance of the 'whole', Gestalt theorists say that more effective learning occurs when the learner can experience the whole skill. They therefore propose that in skill learning it is better to present the whole skill and then break it down, rather than to build it up in stages. Hence the learner can experience the whole skill, and can then focus on parts of the skill which need more work. These weaker areas will vary from learner to learner, so learning of the skill will reflect an individual's own particular style and strengths and the individual can develop his or her own understanding of how to achieve the skill. Thus, there is personal meaning in the learning and performance of the skill.

Insight learning

One of the proposals in Gestalt theory is that we may have a number of experiences which are related, but we do not see that relationship until suddenly it all 'comes together'. This is known as insight learning. For example, a batsman who is struggling against a spin bowler might suddenly have an image of Alec Stewart batting successfully against Shane Warne in a Test Match. He adopts Stewart's approach to the ball and starts to play successful attacking strokes. He was probably not aware of solving his problem by deciding to search his memory for an image of successful batting – it all seemed to happen instantaneously and without conscious effort.

Insight learning is valuable in a sports setting because problems arise in the course of performance which the athlete has to cope with quickly and sometimes alone, and it is a skill which coaches can encourage. They can do this by offering hints to help players make connections (or transfers) between a past experience and the present situation. The hints may relate to the similarity of movements or of situations.

TRANSFER OF LEARNING

Transfer of learning occurs when something learned in one situation has an effect on learning in another situation. For example, tennis players may learn squash skills (which also involve judging the bounce of a ball, eye–hand–racket co-ordination, fast reactions) more rapidly than those who have never played a racket sport.

Positive and negative transfer

If a tennis player learns squash skills fairly rapidly, this is *positive transfer* because the earlier learning has a *beneficial* effect on the later learning. However, if the earlier learning has a *damaging* effect on later learning, *negative transfer* occurs. For example, when a tennis player learns badminton she may play with a straight arm and not use her wrist, so it will take longer for her to use her wrist correctly than it would for a non-tennis player.

A positive transfer is obviously desirable, and it is more likely to occur when:

- the performer is motivated and understands the principles of transfer;
- the tasks have been carefully analysed so that the component parts of the two tasks are similar;

- the points of similarity are stressed for the learner;
- the learning conditions are the same;
- the new task is easier than the first task.

Bilateral transfer

So far, we have considered transfer of learning from one task to another. However, bilateral transfer relates to the transfer of learning between limbs. Research shows that learning can transfer from one muscle group to another, although quite how this occurs is not known. One proposal is that practising a skill with one limb (such as dribbling a basketball with the right hand) creates a generalised motor programme which can then be used by the opposite limb, so when dribbling with the left hand, we adapt this generalised motor programme.

Research confirms that practising with one limb improves performance by the non-practising limb, whether dribbling a basketball or kicking a soccer ball.

FIGURE 3.3 *According to the evidence of bilateral transfer, this player's use of his left foot will improve performance with his right foot*

THE RELATIONSHIP BETWEEN LEARNING AND PERFORMANCE

Before we move on to consider effective skill learning, it is useful to think first about how we assess whether learning has taken place. Learning is an internal process which leads to relatively permanent changes in behaviour as a result of experience or practice. Because learning itself cannot be measured directly, we judge whether a skill has been learned by watching its performance. In other words, performance, which is the execution of a specific motor skill which can be seen and measured, is an indicator of learning.

Performance is not an exact measure of learning though; the athlete may perform poorly even when the skill is well learned. Factors (also called variables) which interfere with performance include fatigue, boredom and arousal. (For more details on the relationship between arousal and performance, see Chapter 4, Arousal, Anxiety and Stress in Performance, p. 93.) Nevertheless, performance measures are useful indicators when used in conjunction with other measures of learning. If performance is measured over a period of time, we can see how it changes and thus assess how successfully the learner has learned. These measurements of performance can be shown on a performance curve.

Performance curves

A performance curve is a graph; all performance curves have the same basic features, as can be seen from the four graphs in Figure 3.4. The horizontal axis is the measure of time or trials, for example after every ten practices, or once a week. The measure of *performance*, such as height, length, number of baskets, is represented against the vertical axis which goes up the side of the graph. By taking these measures over a fixed time, or number of trials, and charting them on the graph, we can see changes in performance and from these infer that there are similar changes in learning. From figure 3.4 you can see the inferences we would make from four different graphs.

These four curves are perfect examples; in reality, a coach who takes such performance measures will find that the curve is more angular. However, many will show what appears to be a levelling off in performance which lasts for a period of time. The reason for this plateau, and its importance for the learner and coach, will be looked at below.

The learning plateau

Singer (1980) proposed that the plateau, or levelling off in performance, may occur while the performer is moving from one stage of skill performance to

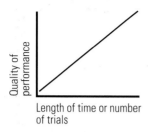

Length of time or number
of trials

A Linear curve
*Steady improvement in performance for
each unit of time or number of trials*

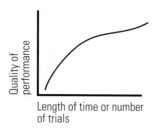

Length of time or number
of trials

B Negatively accelerated curve
*Large amounts of improvement in the
beginning which level off later on*

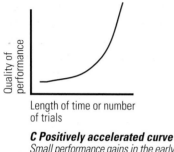

Length of time or number
of trials

C Positively accelerated curve
*Small performance gains in the early stages
which rapidly increase later on*

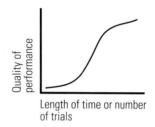

Length of time or number
of trials

D Ogive or S-shaped curve
*Small performance gains followed by steady
improvement which levels off later on*

FIGURE 3.4 *Four types of performance curve*

the next, and during this time the performer may be consolidating his or her knowledge. However, the plateau may also be due to problems in the teaching of the skill, or in the performer's approach. Singer has proposed some of these causes and solutions to the learning plateau:

- **loss of interest or motivation**: make practices more interesting and varied; be enthusiastic and encouraging; provide reinforcement;
- **tiredness or lack of confidence**: slow the rate of teaching; stop practising or practise something else; provide support;
- **lack of understanding**: if directions are not clear or the performer is focussing on the wrong cues, this can be remedied by ensuring that the tasks are small and are made clear, helping the learner attend to the correct cues, providing appropriate feedback.

These solutions are examined in more detail below, as we consider ways in which teachers and coaches can help sportspeople to learn skills more effectively.

MAKING SKILL
LEARNING MORE EFFECTIVE

So far, we have considered some of the explanations for how we learn. In the previous chapter we looked at the information-processing approach and here we have reviewed associationist and several other theories. In the remainder of this chapter we will use these ideas to consider how we can help learners to acquire skills more effectively. To do this, the teacher or coach has to take account of the following factors when organising teaching:

- the purpose of the teaching;
- the skills which are to be taught;
- the abilities and motivation of the learners;
- the resources available – time, space, equipment.

With these factors in mind, we will consider some of the ways in which skills can be taught effectively.

Practices and training

Although practice may indeed 'make perfect', much of the evidence suggests that what is important is how good the practice is (the quality), not how much of it there is (quantity). Baddeley and Longman (1978) found that the typists who practised more than others did not perform any better than the others. This suggests that practice can be tiring and lead to boredom and lower motivation, and is linked to the plateau in the performance curve (see p. 73) and Hull's notion of inhibition (see p. 69). How best can coaches ensure that there is quality in the practices they devise?

Practice has been classified in two ways, according to how a skill is broken down in order to be learned (the method of practice), and according to the type of practice. We look at these topics in some detail in Chapter 2, Analysing and Performing Skills, where we consider types of skills and how we process the information which is necessary in order to perform a skill. Page numbers are given where reference is made below to details contained in Chapter 2, or earlier in this chapter.

Methods of practice

According to the Gestalt view (see p. 70), learning is most effective when the learner has the opportunity to experience a skill in its entirety – the whole method. Critics argue that there is often just too much for the learner to take in at once, and therefore a better method is to break the skill down into smaller units, or parts, and to teach them one at a time. Research suggests that both views have some value, but that the best method is the one most suited to the learner's ability and the type of skill being learned. We will look at the various methods and consider when they might be most appropriate.

The whole method

In the whole method, the learner performs the skill as a complete unit, perhaps having seen it demonstrated first. This gives the learner a feel for the whole movement (proprioceptive information, see p. 41) and how the various subroutines relate to each other so that it can be performed. Skills that have to be performed rapidly (stopping a ball) are best practised as a whole, because breaking them down into parts, or subroutines (see p. 35), might radically change the movement and thus make it *harder* to perform as a whole. This method is also suitable for fairly simple skills (catching a netball) because they do not make many demands on the learner's attention (see p. 42). It is also less time consuming for teacher and learner.

The part method

If a skill is long (a gymnastic routine) or complex (hurdling) and can be broken down into sections, the part method will be useful. This entails practising each part of the skill until it is well learned, then putting the parts together to make a whole. However, though it may be appropriate to teach a skill in parts, one of the difficulties is that the learner still has to put the parts together to make a whole, so chaining (see below) may be preferable.

The whole–part–whole method

This enables the learner to experience the skill as a whole, then to practise aspects of it, and then to re-combine the parts into performance of the whole skill. This is also useful if only one part of the skill requires attention – it can be practised until it is performed as well as the other parts and then re-integrated. This is why it is valuable to finish a training session with a practice of the whole skill.

Chaining or the progressive part method

Too much emphasis on the parts can cause problems when the learner tries to integrate the parts into the whole. Certain skills, particularly those which are long and complex such as gymnastic routines, are best learned in stages which are linked together because the successful start of each stage depends on the accurate completion of the previous one. Thus, the links between the stages are learned at the same time as the stages.

Questions which the coach should ask in order to determine the best method of practice are:

- **How continuous is the skill?** When a skill is continuous (see p. 35) – when the end of one part of it forms the beginning of the next, as in cycling or skating – it is not possible to break it down so it must be taught as a whole.
- **How coherent is the skill?** For example, netball passing can be split into

parts (jump, catch, land, pivot, throw) each of which is relatively coherent or self-contained (see p. 35). In a tennis serve, the throw and racket stroke, though separate skills, are performed at the same time by the same parts of the body, so the serve is one coherent (whole) skill.

■ **How much information can the learner cope with?** If the learner can remember long sequences (which require good attention and memory) then the whole method may be better. The skilled sportsperson should be able to benefit from the whole method, whereas the novice or the younger learner is likely to have limited abilities to attend and remember so the part method may be preferable. Simple skills involve less processing capacity (see p. 42) than complex skills, and therefore are more easily learned as a whole.

FIGURE 3.5 *What method of practice is most appropriate for these speedskaters?*

Types of practice

There are three types of practice, each has its advantages and disadvantages, and they are discussed below.

■ **massed practice,** where a skill is practised repeatedly over an extended period of time. Skills will not be forgotten, but there is a risk of boredom, overtraining, inhibition or fatigue. Massed practice is more valuable for the more experienced, older or fitter player.

■ **distributed practice**, where sessions are short and spaced with periods of rest or a change in activities occurs between practice sessions. This prevents fatigue or boredom setting in, but there is a risk that some of the learning will be forgotten between practices. This is useful for younger learners who may have a short concentration span or for less fit players.

- **variable practice**, which includes both types, but which one is used will depend on the nature of the skill, the motivation and ability of the players, the time available and other relevant factors.

For example, the tennis player of national ranking may use massed practice to improve the footwork on his backhand drive – he is highly motivated and wants to reach the skill level at which the drive is performed automatically and accurately under extreme pressure. In contrast, the average club player who is attending a coaching session may see a demonstration of the shot and have a short practice with feedback from the coach. He then goes away and practises the shot now and then when he has the opportunity, which is an example of distributed practice.

Introducing variety into the content and sequence of practice drills reduces tedium and boredom. A valuable technique in team sports is to give players a chance to play in different positions. This enables them to use other skills whilst increasing their understanding of other positions and team members' skills.

Demonstrating skills

We have already noted the role of observational learning and now we can examine how the teacher or coach can demonstrate most effectively, using Bandura's (1977a) ideas on modelling (see p. 69). Bandura proposed that there are four stages in the modelling process. These are described below, together with ways in which they can be used by coaches.

1 **attention**: the performer attends to particular information, so the coach needs to highlight the important elements of a skill in order to help the performer attend to what is most relevant. When beginning to learn a skill, for example, the performer is frequently overwhelmed by a mass of information so the coach acts as a guide to the key features. At a more advanced stage, the coach may focus on the relationship between particular features of the skill and how they affect a particular outcome.

2 **retention**: the learner must retain, or remember, the information in order to reproduce it. Techniques which help retention include repeating key points, making the purpose of a practice clear, making practices meaningful or vivid. For more on improving memory see p. 46.

3 **motor reproduction**: the performer must be physically capable of performing the skill, even though practice and feedback are required. To help in the physical performance of the skill, the coach may use aids for support or safety (such as a harness in trampolining) or use physical guidance (gently holding the ankles in a headstand).

4 **motivation**: the coach can motivate the performer through the use of social reinforcements such as encouragement or praise, or through goal setting (see Chapter 6, Maintaining Participation and Improving Performance, p. 153).

Observational learning involves the use of cognitive skills of the kind discussed in Chapter 2 under the information-processing approach. Coaches act as models for others, in their behaviour, dress, attitudes and of course as demonstrators of skills. Coaches are constantly communicating messages to learners – about how difficult the skill is, how enthusiastic they are, how confident they are in the learners' ability and so on. Nevertheless, there are number of factors which can affect the usefulness of the demonstration, according to observational learning. These mean that learning may not be quite as we expect. Let us look briefly at two examples.

■ **skill level**: research by Landers and Landers (1973) with adolescent girls on a balancing task showed that performance improved after they had seen the task done by a skilled teacher, but that performance by a skilled peer had little impact. However, after observing an *unskilled peer*, performance also improved. One explanation is that observing a skilled peer can de-motivate a learner because it highlights the discrepancy in their abilities, whereas seeing an unskilled peer is motivating because the youngster thinks 'Well at least I can do better than that'.

■ **sex of teacher**: although Bandura has shown that we are more likely to model those who are similar to us, for example if they are the same sex, research in a sports setting does not always bear out this prediction. For example, despite having female teachers to teach sport and PE in schools, there is still a decline in interest and participation amongst adolescent girls. Equally, despite few same-sex models in sports such as football and rugby, girls are participating in these sports in greater numbers.

Forms of guidance

The purpose of guidance is to help learners to acquire and perform a new skill as effectively as possible. Information provided by the coach or teacher is communicated through the senses – what the learner sees, hears and feels. We will therefore consider guidance which is visual, verbal or manual/mechanical.

Visual guidance

This is valuable at any stage of learning, but particularly in the very early stages. Visual guidance offers the learner a model of the skill or movement which is to be learned. When a teacher demonstrates a shot, a pass or a movement, the learner is able to see the skill as a whole and to retain the image in memory. Vision is the most powerful of the senses, it is the most direct and can be the easiest to remember. We have seen that in demonstrating a skill the teacher's role is to point out which aspects of the skill to take note of. For the more skilled sportsperson, a demonstration can highlight specific problems and their solutions.

Other forms of visual guidance include charts, diagrams, videos, markers and models. They can be used for many purposes such as:

- providing feedback on a learner's performance – by marking a court or placing a box to see how many balls, bags or shuttles land on target, by making and showing a video of their performance;
- to teach positioning or tactics – using a model or drawn diagram of a pitch or court to show how players should move in relation to each other or to change from a defensive to an attacking formation;
- to form images which help the learner retain information in memory – through charts or diagrams (still images) or videos to show body shape or position or to help the learner focus on a key point which must be remembered.

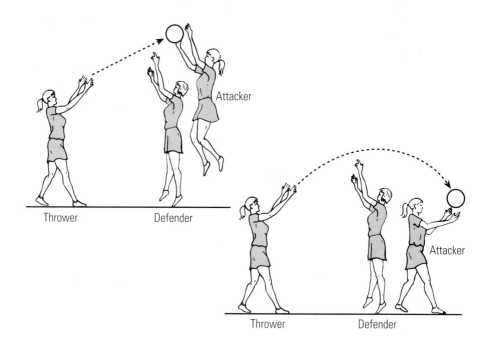

FIGURE 3.6 *This illustration of two types of lob in netball is an example of visual guidance*

Verbal guidance

Verbal guidance may accompany visual guidance or be used alone, for example a teacher providing feedback on a movement or a coach directing players' positions in a practice session. The teacher may use key words to guide a player, and to help players guide themselves in future. So an instruction to 'Step, swing' reminds the player to focus on footwork and arm action when striking the ball.

As was seen in Chapter 2 under the information-processing approach, we are only able to hear, understand and remember a limited amount of spoken information at one time, so the coach must use verbal guidance carefully, particularly when teaching novices. Verbal guidance should be:

- **clear** – using short and simple words which are easy to understand and are spoken distinctly, emphasising key words;
- **short** – so that only a few 'bits' of information are communicated;
- **relevant** – to the learner's ability to understand, remember and perform the skill;
- **translatable** – easy for the learner to transform what is said into the desired action. Verbal guidance may be more effective for the advanced performer whose knowledge of the sport enables him or her to translate verbal information into visual images more easily.

An additional problem is that verbal guidance may be inadequate to communicate the subtleties of a movement or the complexities of a tactic. This is where *visual* guidance is more valuable: it can be used to highlight a key point or to demonstrate a sequence of moves.

Manual/mechanical guidance

This is physical guidance which provides confidence or safety whilst a skill is being learned or to give the learner a sense of the skill being learned. Mechanical guidance is provided by equipment, such as a back float in swimming, whereas manual guidance is provided when the coach, for example, covers the learner's hands on a hockey stick to help her learn the hit. Such guidance can aid the learner in one of two ways:

- **Supporting movements** through manual or mechanical guidance: this enables the learner to develop skills and confidence while reducing the risk of damage. A gymnast trying a backward roll off the box may be supported by the teacher (manual guidance) for the first few attempts until her skill level and confidence improve. Whether the learner uses manual guidance or mechanical guidance, teachers must ensure that these 'crutches' are removed as soon as possible or the learner may become dependent and fail to gain both kinaesthetic awareness and confidence. For example, the child who learns to swim using a back float does not feel the proper relationship between his muscle activity, the pressure of the water and his

movement in the water until the float is removed.
■ **Directing movement** such as holding the beginner's hands on the cricket bat and striking the ball may give the learner some sense of the timing of the action and the necessary co-ordination of movements, but because he neither initiates nor performs the action, this directing of movements is of limited value. The learner does not 'feel' the weight of the bat, does not initiate the movement in shoulders and forearm, or co-ordinate this with the transfer of weight.

FIGURE 3.7 *Ian Botham using manual guidance to help a novice cricketer*

Guidance and learning styles

We have seen a number of ways in which a teacher can communicate information to the learner, but research shows that we each tend to have a preferred style of learning. For example, some people can take in visual and verbal information at the same time, others can only handle one of these at a time. Some people learn best by watching and doing, others by doing and then listening. For the teacher of a large group, this can be problematic, but the best way of teaching is to ensure that all three forms of guidance are used where possible. In smaller groups, or with individuals, the ability to identify a learner's preferred learning style will enable the teacher to present information in the most effective way for that individual.

APPLICATION
The coach's role in guidance

- Make it clear and precise.
- Ensure it can be seen and/or heard by every learner.
- Keep it simple and brief.
- Highlight key features of the skill or movement.

- Make it appropriate to the learner.
- Teach basic skills before moving on to more complex ones.
- Maintain variety in the activities and pace of the instruction.

Feedback

Feedback is the information that tells us about movements we have made. It is valuable because it can motivate, reward and improve the performance of an athlete. It is most effective when it is precise and specific because it provides information on the success or failure of a particular movement. It appears that regardless of successful or unsuccessful performance, a high level of feedback corresponds to high levels of enjoyment and perceived success. When asked about Gerry Francis' feedback as a manager of Bristol Rovers, a defender commented:

> 'He had this remarkable ability to improve players irrespective of where they played. He noticed everything. It was as if he had a video camera running in his head and he could freeze-frame incidents after the match, things you might not even have remembered yourself.'
>
> (from the *Independent on Sunday*, 21.1.96.)

On p. 51 we consider different types of feedback and how we use this feedback to learn skills. A coach can make skill learning more effective by providing two types of feedback:

- **Knowledge of results** relates to the results or outcome of an action, and may be directly available to the athlete, who can see, for example, whether a shot misses the goal. However, coaches can often provide additional information such as the lap time or the path of a ball.
- **Knowledge of performance** relates to the way in which a movement is carried out, and can be provided by a video or comments by the coach. Feedback about performance is particularly valuable to the athlete because research suggests that performers are often unable to identify which aspects of their movement are improving and which are not, or the position of their limbs at a particular point in performance.

The amount and timing of feedback can affect how useful the feedback is to the performer:

83

- **Quantity**: the learner can only absorb a small amount of feedback at any one time and therefore coaches need to be sensitive to how much feedback the learner can use. For more skilled sportspeople, awareness of how much feedback they can use is equally important: individuals differ in their ability to make sense of and use information – whether verbal or visual.
- **Timing**: feedback can be provided whilst the skill is being performed, for example the coach might run alongside a hurdler to tell her how high she lifts her leading knee. This is called *concurrent* feedback and it can be given by the coach, a fellow player or individuals to themselves. Our hurdler might continue her training session by 'feeling' the height of her knee as she approaches the hurdle. Another example of concurrent feedback is split times, which provide the swimmer or runner with feedback about their time during their performance. Feedback which is given at the end of a performance is known as *terminal* feedback.

When providing feedback the coach should also include information about the next step, so that the feedback provides a link between a performed skill and how to modify or extend it. A netball coach may say to a player after a poor throw 'That footwork's good but your throw needs more accuracy. Remember to follow through.'

Teaching styles

There are a number of ways of presenting information to others. Effective learning involves keeping the learner motivated, promoting enjoyment and encouraging achievement. To do this the teacher needs to be aware of factors such as the age of the learners, their experience, their reasons for learning, and what is to be learned in order to adopt the teaching style which should lead to the most effective learning.

Mosston and Ashworth (1986) have looked at the roles of the teacher and the learner in this process. They propose that teaching and learning involve decisions about what is taught/learned, when, how, and so on. The amount of influence the teacher and learner each has on these decisions can be classified and labelled on their Spectrum of Teaching Styles. At one end of the spectrum the teacher makes all the decisions (the command style), at the other end the learner makes most of them (the discovery style). We will look at four of the styles on this spectrum whilst considering the circumstances in which they are appropriate, their strengths and weaknesses.

Command style

Here, the teacher has an authoritarian role and the command style can be used to control a group (such as a class of primary school children) or convey the same information to all participants (for example in an aerobics group). All learners are treated in the same way and have very little influence on what is taught or how it is taught. Learners copy the teacher's behaviour or instructions and there is little opportunity for social contact between learners. The command style of teaching is used in drill training, which is described earlier in this chapter on p. 66. Its advantages and disadvantages are shown in Table 3.1.

Table 3.1 The advantages and disadvantages of the command style of teaching

Advantages	Disadvantages
it is an effective way of demonstrating a simple skill or one which is being taught for the first time	discourages the learner from thinking about what is taught, and from questioning
gives clear information (on movements, skills or tactics, for example)	discourages the learner from developing responsibility for their own learning and so developing qualities which aid intrinsic motivation
establishes clear relationships and routines	is of limited use when developing open skills, which require the learner to make their own decisions and to adapt
enables the teacher to monitor and maintain the safety of learners	makes it difficult for learners to solve their own problems in performing the skill
enables the teacher to control behaviour, what is taught, and how available time is used	reduces the opportunity for affiliation and social contact, which are reasons why people undertake and enjoy sports
	provides little opportunity for the teacher to supply individualised feedback or extrinsic rewards where appropriate
	may hamper the skill development of the most able and deter the less able

Reciprocal (or paired) style

This style allows learners to participate more actively in their learning. The teacher decides what is to be taught, but learners work together in pairs, taking turns to be a performer and an observer. This allows each one to observe and analyse the other's performances and provide instant feedback. Everyone needs to know exactly what to do and should have some basic skills. The teacher's role here is to monitor what is happening, to give advice or support or to correct if necessary. However, it requires careful monitoring to ensure that what the teacher has planned is being put into effect. Advantages and disadvantages are listed in Table 3.2.

Table 3.2 The advantages and disadvantages of the reciprocal style of teaching

Advantages	Disadvantages
encourages the learner to take responsibility for their own learning	puts considerable demands on the teacher to monitor each pairing – what is happening, and the understanding of the learners
encourages the development of communication and of more advanced skills, such as the analysis of movement	may encourage faulty techniques and learning if the learners' knowledge is limited and incorrect feedback is given
provides instant feedback	depends on a reasonable level of development of the learners, so they can analyse and communicate clearly and tactfully so that comments are not taken personally
enhances self-confidence	

Problem-solving style

Here, the teacher sets problems for the learners to solve, which encourages learners to think about their sport and to be creative in their approach to problems. There may be only one solution or several, and the teacher may have limited control over how the learners work and think in order to solve the problem.

This style is useful when there may be a number of possible options or when the teacher wishes the learners to use information they have already learned but to apply and evaluate it in a novel situation; this encourages transfer of learning. For example, the teacher may ask 'How could you gain the attack if you were in this situation?'. Learners may benefit from hearing others explain their ideas or understanding, just as it helps their own understanding when they have to articulate their ideas and explain their thinking to others. In this way the learner develops a deeper knowledge and understanding of a skill or activity by seeing it from different perspectives and therefore eventually more as a 'whole'. The learner needs to have some experience within the sport, hence the problem-solving style is appropriate for the more skilled performer. Advantages and disadvantages are shown in Table 3.3.

Table 3.3 The advantages and disadvantages of the problem-solving style of teaching

Advantages	Disadvantages
increases understanding which in turn increases motivation	requires learners who are able and confident about expressing themselves
may be used with an individual or with a group or team	can be time-consuming
is valuable in circumstances where the sportsperson has to make their own decisions whilst the competitive situation is in progress	it is difficult for the teacher to know just what has been learned
helps the learner develop their own solutions to problems	requires the teacher to have an extensive knowledge of the topic

Discovery style

In this style of teaching the teacher guides the learner by giving clues, hints and questions which get the learner to 'discover' ways of improving a skill or strategy. For example, the teacher might say 'Try it with your weight on the front foot, then with your weight equally distributed. Which is most effective? What situation could you use it in?'. Here, the teacher is a facilitator. There are similarities between this and the previous style, but discovery style is a more creative and open-ended approach, and it is particularly appropriate to creative dance and some aspects of outdoor activities. The advantages and disadvantages of the discovery style are similar to those of the problem-solving style, but there are some additional points, as shown in Table 3.4.

Table 3.4 The advantages and disadvantages of the discovery style of teaching

Advantages	Disadvantages
enhances self-confidence	is very time-consuming
is most valuable in activities where there are a variety of options and where creativity is a key feature	needs to be tailored to each performer's level of development and abilities

As the teaching style moves from teacher centred to learner centred, so the learner has greater control over and involvement with his or her learning. This has benefits in that it increases individual self-efficacy (see p. 165), enables the learner to remember and use learned skills more effectively, and increases interpersonal skills. However, it is only appropriate with certain age groups, certain abilities, and in certain group sizes. A good teacher will be skilled in the full range of teaching styles and will deploy them appropriately.

FIGURE 3.8 *When working with children, make it brief and visual*

Teaching and coaching children

There are references to teaching children throughout this book, but here are some of the key points which those who teach or coach children should keep in mind to make their learning more effective:

- make information short and simple because children have a brief attention span and short memories;
- stress visual information because it is noticed and remembered more effectively than verbal information;
- give plenty of opportunities to be active: after demonstrating a skill let the children try it out as soon as possible, in a variety of ways, and often;
- keep practices, fun, varied and active;
- structure the teaching of skills carefully so that the basic skills can be learned and developed, then the learning of newer and more complex skills will be more easily achieved;
- emphasise mastery of simple skills for under 6s. Restrict the competitive element of sports activities for older children and encourage children to develop performance-related rather than outcome-related goals. Do this by helping them set performance goals and by praising effort and performance rather than results. Encourage co-operation rather than competition;

- use reinforcement generously and appropriately, especially for slow learners, the novice or those surrounded by much more able youngsters, but encourage the development of intrinsic motivation;
- provide for successful experiences (short tennis, positive feedback, appropriate goals, appropriate competition) and ensure young players are aware of their achievement;
- avoid punishment;
- allow children some involvement in decision making as it is a powerful motivator;
- be patient: the child is more important than the activity.

CHAPTER SUMMARY

This chapter has continued the theme of the previous chapter by introducing several more explanations for how we learn skills. Some explanations propose that learning occurs as an association develops between a stimulus and a response, others take greater account of the individual's understanding. We have noted that performance is not a true indication of learning, and that the rate of learning can be uneven. We have considered ways in which coaches can make skill learning more effective by tailoring their practices, training and teaching styles to the skills to be learned, to the individual differences in ability and, in particular, to children.

chapter four

CHAPTER OVERVIEW

The pressure of competition can pep up and improve an individual's performance or damage it. For most of us, competition is associated with feeling alert and ready, yet we may also experience apprehension, sweating palms or worry about how we will perform. If we can find out why this happens, how we can prevent the ill-effects and harness the positive aspects, then we should be able to improve performance. This chapter first examines how and why these effects occur and ends by considering ways of controlling them in performance.

THE RELATIONSHIP BETWEEN AROUSAL, ANXIETY AND STRESS

As sportspeople, we are interested in situations in which a performer's concerns about his or her situation lead to damaging outcomes, perhaps poor performance or a display of aggression. The same situation however may produce improved performance in another athlete. The process through which this occurs is called the *stress process*, an illustration of which is shown in Figure 4.1.

You will see that the terms arousal, anxiety and stress appear in Figure 4.1; in fact these three terms are often used as though they mean much the same thing. In an effort to gain a better understanding, psychologists have tried to differentiate between them, although this is not easy as there is so much overlap between these terms. However they can be defined in the following ways:

- **arousal** refers to the state of alertness and anticipation that prepares the body for action: it involves physiological activity (such as increased heart rate) and cognitive activity (such as an increase in attention);
- **anxiety** is a vague form of fear or apprehension that is created by awareness of this arousal: it is a negative emotional state, caused because a situation is seen as threatening;

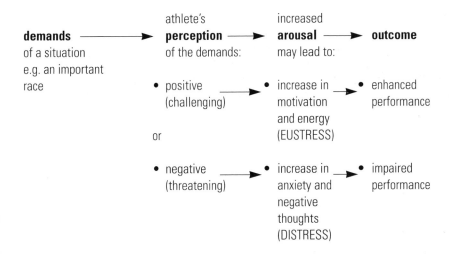

FIGURE 4.1 *A basic model of the stress process*

■ **stress** is sometimes used to refer to the whole process (as in Figure 4.1), but is also used in a more specific way. Stress is what results when performers see themselves as unable to meet the demands of a situation. As you can see from Figure 4.1, this is actually called *distress* but it is usually shortened to *stress*. A definition of stress which is generally accepted is provided by Lazarus and Folkman (1984). You can see that it includes the points we have just covered:

> 'Stress is a pattern of negative physiological states and psychological responses occurring in situations where people perceive threats to their well-being which they may be unable to meet.'

Kremer and Scully (1994) are amongst the psychologists who have argued that separating arousal, anxiety and stress is too tidy because there is considerable overlap and interaction between them. Nevertheless, it does help to consider them one at a time, whilst highlighting ways in which they overlap. We will start by examining arousal, which is neither positive nor negative; it is the *perception* of that arousal which may lead to anxiety and stress. Therefore, when we move on to look at anxiety and stress we also consider their negative effects on performance.

AROUSAL

Arousal is a physiological state of alertness and anticipation which prepares the body for action. It refers to the activation of both the body and the mind and in itself is neither good nor bad. We need a degree of activation to function effectively, whether to digest a meal or to catch a cricket ball. When catching a cricket ball, the player is responding to an external stimulus and it is a stimulus such as this, which creates a demand on the individual, that interests sports psychologists. To perform to the best of our ability, we need to be in the appropriate state of activation (not too little, not too much). However, sometimes we seem to be over-aroused, and this often damages our performance. In order to control arousal, therefore, we need to understand how it works.

How does the body become aroused?

When a batsman hits a cricket ball, the fielders interpret what they see and respond accordingly. Physiologically they will already be in a state of activation as the bowler runs up, because they are alert and prepared to respond to the strike of the ball. However, if the ball sails in the air towards a fielder, he will experience increased arousal as he moves towards the ball to take the catch. What is going on in his body to enable him to do all this?

The part of the brain which has a major role in regulating arousal is the *reticular activating system*. This is part of the brain stem, which links the spinal cord with the forebrain (where activities such as thinking, perception, information about body position and monitoring of blood flow all take place). Thus, the reticular activating system is involved in organising sensory–motor behaviour through its interconnections between the brain and the limbs. It is activated by changes in the information we receive and thus helps us respond to new situations, such as when fielding a cricket ball.

Another part of the brain, the *hypothalamus*, also plays a part in the regulation of consciousness and activates the *autonomic nervous system*. The autonomic nervous system is sometimes called the centre for the emotions; it regulates internal bodily processes such as heartbeat, breathing and digestion. It does this through its two parts:

- the **sympathetic division**, which stimulates the body and causes it to expend energy;
- the **parasympathetic division**, which conserves energy.

When activated, the sympathetic division mobilises the body for an emergency. It *increases* heart and breathing rates, muscles tense, perspiration increases to cool the body and sugar is released into the bloodstream to provide more energy. This pattern of increased action, the 'flight or fight' response, is the *arousal reaction*.

Once the emergency is over, the parasympathetic division acts to counteract the effect of the 'flight or fight' response and bring bodily functions back into balance. For example, activation of the parasympathetic division *slows* breathing and heart rate and increases digestion.

The effect of arousal on the mind and the body

The above is a very simple description of the brain's arousal processes, but it does refer to the three types of arousal identified by Lacey (1967), namely arousal of:

- **the mind** (electrocortical arousal) – the degree of electrical activity in the cortex, measured by electroencephalogram (EEG) – which is evident in an increase in attention, faster processing of information, confused thinking and difficulty in concentrating;
- **the body** (autonomic arousal) – the degree of physiological activity in the autonomic nervous system, measured by skin conductance, heart rate, blood pressure – which is evident in a pounding heart or sweating palms;
- **behaviour** – observable activity such as hands which shake, restless pacing, blood draining from the face.

The way that these types of arousal interact is complex. Lacey showed that it was possible for activity in one system to be high whilst in another system it was low, and that different tasks triggered different patterns of activity. For example in behaviour involving reaction time (such as saving a penalty in soccer) heart rate is lowered but skin conductance is usually raised. When stressful cognitive activity is involved, such as deciding how to play a difficult shot at golf, both of these are usually lowered.

What is the relationship between arousal and performance?

Arousal is neutral; it is the activation of the system. Some level of activation is necessary for action, yet too much can be detrimental. Consider these two accounts of arousal and performance (Hemery, 1986):

- Ed Moses, gold medal winner in the 400 m hurdles at the 1976 and 1984 Olympics says

  'The way I get the best out is by not expecting an easy race. It's easier when there's pressure. You get emotional and go out to perform' (p. 163).

- Bob Tisdall described a fellow student at Cambridge who desperately wanted to win a race for the university in order to get a 'blue' and who stayed on for a fourth year especially to have another chance. Tisdall reported that the student 'froze in the starting blocks in the finals. We had to pick him up and he was stiff, like a corpse' (p. 131).

Ed Moses consciously created arousal in order to achieve optimum performance. Arousal here has a positive effect, whereas for the student it had a negative effect on performance. Let us review some explanations for these two effects before we look at the impact of particular factors on performance.

Drive theory

One of the earliest descriptions of the relationship between arousal and performance was that as an individual's *arousal* increases, his or her *performance* improves. This relationship is known as a linear one because it is represented by a straight line, which can be seen from Figure 4.2. The relationship can be shown as:

performance = arousal × skill level

This is known as drive theory, which was developed by Hull (1951) and Spence (1956), and a key component is the performer's level of ability in a skill. If a skill or task is well learned then arousal, such as in competition, will enable the performer to produce the skill very successfully. However, if the performer's skill level is low, then arousal will damage the performance and he or she is likely to produce an even worse performance when aroused. In other words, arousal seems to exaggerate the performer's ability.

Critics of drive theory argue that what is a 'well-learned task' is hard to define. It is even more difficult to test in a real-life setting because many tasks contain both well-learned and novel elements. In addition, evidence from many situations suggested that beyond a certain level of arousal, the individual's performance often deteriorates, even on well-learned tasks. An extreme example is the student athlete who 'froze' on the starting blocks.

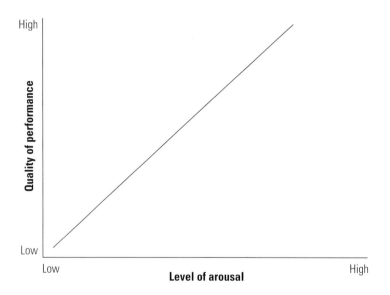

FIGURE 4.2 *Graph showing relationship between arousal and performance according to drive theory*

Inverted-U hypothesis

This explanation accounts for some of the criticisms of drive theory. It is based on the Yerkes–Dodson Law, which predicts the relationship between arousal and quality of performance. The inverted-U hypothesis states that arousal causes an increase in performance, but only up to a point – called the optimal point. As arousal increases beyond that point, performance *deteriorates*. When a sportsperson's level of arousal and quality of performance are measured, then plotted on a graph, it is shaped like an inverted 'U' (Figure 4.3).

It can be seen from Figure 4.3 that performance is at its best (optimal) when there is a moderate level of arousal. Research has shown that this inverted-U relationship exists in a number of different circumstances, which are reviewed briefly below.

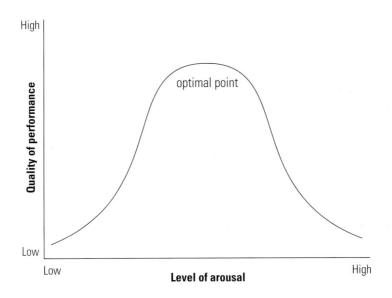

FIGURE 4.3 *Graph showing the inverted-U relationship between arousal and performance*

Types of skill
Oxendine (1970) found an inverted-U relationship in several sports, but noted that the amount of arousal necessary for optimal performance depended on the nature of the skill. This is illustrated in Figure 4.4, which shows, for example, that optimal performance when putting in golf requires a low level of arousal, whereas tackling in football requires a high level of arousal. Oxendine proposed that more complex skills (putting in golf) need *less* arousal for optimal performance because high arousal interferes with fine

muscle movement, co-ordination and cognitive activities such as concentration. However, high arousal is useful in less complex skills requiring strength, endurance and speed, such as tackling in football.

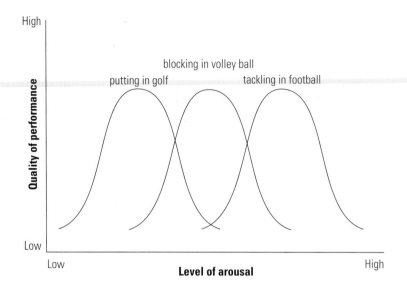

FIGURE 4.4 *Graph showing the relationship between level of arousal and level of performance in three skills*

Critics such as Jones and Hardy (1990) argue that many skills involve both strength *and* complexity, which are difficult to separate out. For example, if a golfer was preparing to putt, an appropriate activation state would include low muscle activity in the forearms but high cognitive activity. However, performing a maximum bench press in the weights gymnasium would require high muscle activity and lower cognitive activity.

Arousal can be more damaging to the performance of open skills than of closed skills because open skills are performed in an unpredictable environment so they make more cognitive demands on the performer. For example, when receiving and passing a basketball, the player must simultaneously judge the flight of the ball, the movement of team-mates and opposition on court, and make decisions about tactics whilst performing complex motor skills.

Level of expertise
Research also shows that someone who is just learning a sport needs only very low levels of arousal to perform well. Additional arousal, such as occurs when being watched, leads to a deterioration in performance. In contrast, the

elite performer will find that such low-level arousal would have no effect on performance. He or she will need much higher levels in order to produce ·optimal performance. An explanation for this lies in Fitts and Posner's (1967) description of the first phase of skill learning – the cognitive phase (see p. 61). Because control of the skill is not yet automatic, the learner uses his or her cognitive abilities to direct, monitor and control the skill. Additional arousal may cause confused thinking which interferes with the ability to control the skill successfully. The inverted-U relationship between arousal and level of expertise is shown in Figure 4.5.

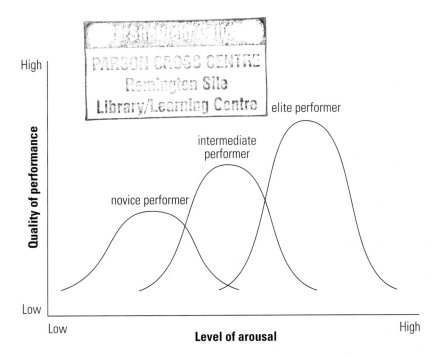

FIGURE 4.5 *Graph showing the relationship between level of arousal and level of expertise*

Personality
In Chapter 1, The Individual in Sport, we looked at Eysenck's theory of personality (p. 14). His introversion–extroversion dimension reflects the amount of arousal the individual needs, which is regulated by the reticular activating system. The introvert quickly experiences over-arousal, and we would presume that the introvert would experience higher anxiety and therefore poorer performance than the extrovert. Research, however, has produced conflicting results.

It is possible that impulsivity (a combination of Eysenck's extraversion and neuroticism) is an important personality variable. Research suggests that those with low impulsivity tend to be more highly aroused during the early part of the day, whilst those with high impulsivity are more highly aroused later in the day. This has particular implications for performance: for example, an athlete rated as high in impulsivity will need to use more relaxation and stress-reduction strategies when running in an evening as compared to a morning race.

Audiences and social facilitation
From Chapter 5 we can see that others may have the effect of improving or impairing our performance (see p. 133 for more details). Zajonc (1965) argued that the presence of other people creates arousal. The explanations offered by other psychologists propose that this is because we may worry about being evaluated by others, or because people create distraction which conflicts with our ability to perform a task on which we are concentrating. Arousal caused by the presence of others may therefore push us past the optimal performance level.

ANXIETY

Although arousal itself is neutral, if it is associated with negative thoughts and feelings then we experience anxiety. This is a negative emotional state associated with feelings such as worry and apprehension. Anxiety may be created by a situation which we see as threatening, perhaps because we doubt our ability to cope with it. Spielberger (1966) called this anxiety response *state anxiety*, which he differentiated from *trait anxiety*. Let us look at these two briefly.

Trait anxiety

Trait anxiety is enduring, it is a personality trait, it is part of the individual's pattern of behaviours. Someone who easily becomes anxious, even about non-threatening situations, has high *trait anxiety*. For example, a sportsperson who worries about the condition of the ground for next month's match would be described as trait anxious. (For more details on the relationship between trait anxiety and personality see Chapter 1, p. 16.) Spielberger (1966) predicts that individuals with high trait anxiety will perceive *more* situations as threatening, and respond to challenges with more *state* anxiety than those who are low trait-anxious individuals.

State anxiety

When you feel apprehensive, tense and short of breath at the start of a race you are experiencing what Spielberger calls *state anxiety*. This is a temporary emotional state, a *response* to a situation which is seen as a threat. It may change with circumstances: for example, at the start of a rugby match a player may feel moderate levels of state anxiety, but once things get under way state anxiety levels drop. However, if the player has to convert a try at a crucial point in the match, then state anxiety levels are likely to rise dramatically. State anxiety has two components:

- **cognitive state anxiety**, which is feelings of nervousness, apprehension and worry;
- **somatic state anxiety**, which is the awareness of arousal in the body.

Some people may show high somatic state anxiety but at the same time be calm and mentally collected – showing low cognitive state anxiety.

Competitive anxiety

Sportspeople can be anxious about many things, such as training schedules, injuries, finances or personal relationships. However the main source of anxiety for sportspeople is thought to be competition, and for this reason the study of *competitive anxiety* (anxiety which occurs in a sports-specific setting) has been of considerable interest to sports psychologists. One such psychologist, Martens (1977), researched *trait* anxiety in a sports setting, which he defined as:

'the tendency to see competitive situations as threatening and to respond with feelings of apprehension or tension.' (p. 23)

When a player who has a high level of *competitive trait anxiety* (is constantly anxious about competing) is in a competitive situation, he or she will experience even more anxiety. This is because the competitive situation creates the perception of threat in the individual (related largely to the threat of being evaluated by others). According to Martens, therefore, high competitive *trait* anxiety will result in high competitive *state* anxiety. He developed the Sport Competition Anxiety Test (SCAT) (Martens, 1977), which asks performers specific questions relating to their feelings in a pre-competitive situation. Responses are scored to give a level of competitive trait anxiety. Figure 4.6 shows an extract from the SCAT, together with the scoring method.

The multidimensional model of anxiety

Earlier, we looked at the relationship between arousal and performance as if arousal is a single concept. However, we know that arousal involves both physiological and cognitive changes. When we looked at anxiety, we saw these differences reflected in the distinction between somatic state and cognitive state anxiety. Let us examine their effect on performance.

Sport Competition Anxiety Test (SCAT)

Directions: Below are some statements about how persons feel when they compete in sports and games. Read each statement and decide if you HARDLY EVER, or SOMETIMES, or OFTEN feel this way when you compete in sports and games. If your choice is HARDLY EVER, blacken the square labeled A; if your choice is SOMETIMES, blacken the square labeled B; and if your choice is OFTEN, blacken the square labeled C. There are no right or wrong answers. Do not spend too much time on any one question. Remember to choose the word that describes how you usually feel when competing in sports and games.

		Hardly ever	Sometimes	Often
1	Competing against others is socially enjoyable.	A ☐	B ☐	C ☐
2	Before I compete I feel uneasy.	A ☐	B ☐	C ☐
3	Before I compete I worry about not performing well.	A ☐	B ☐	C ☐
4	I am a good sportsman when I compete.	A ☐	B ☐	C ☐
5	When I compete I worry about making mistakes.	A ☐	B ☐	C ☐
6	Before I compete I am calm.	A ☐	B ☐	C ☐
7	Setting a goal is important when competing.	A ☐	B ☐	C ☐
8	Before I compete I get a queasy feeling in my stomach.	A ☐	B ☐	C ☐
9	Just before competing I notice my heart beats faster than usual.	A ☐	B ☐	C ☐

How to score the SCAT for adults. For each item three responses are possible: (a) Hardly ever, (b) Sometimes, and (c) Often. The 10 test items are 2, 3, 5, 6, 8 and 9. The spurious items (1, 4 and 7) are not scored. Items 2, 3, 5, 8 and 9 are worded so that they are scored according to the following key:

> 1 = Hardly ever
> 2 = Sometimes
> 3 = Often

Item 6 is scored as follows:

> 1 = Often
> 2 = Sometimes
> 3 = Hardly ever

FIGURE 4.6 *An extract from the Sport Competition Anxiety Test. The higher the score, the higher the level of competitive trait anxiety. (adapted from Martens, 1977)*

Somatic state anxiety

The description of the athlete who 'froze' on the starting blocks is an extreme example of the effect of somatic state anxiety. Many sportspeople show muscle tension or poor co-ordination when they experience high levels of state anxiety. Those who already have a high level of trait anxiety will show more state anxiety than those with low trait anxiety. An example is provided in research such as that by Weinberg and Hunt.

RESEARCH
Weinberg and Hunt (1976)

Students were divided into two groups: one comprised high trait-anxious students and the other low trait-anxious students. Each student was asked to throw tennis balls at a target; the students were observed as they did this and their accuracy was noted. In addition, the students were monitored for electrical activity in their muscles. Results showed that the group with high trait anxiety showed more state anxiety than the other group, and the high trait-anxious students used more muscular energy before, during and after their throws. We can conclude that higher levels of anxiety contributed to increased muscle tension and co-ordination, which in turn interfered with their performance.

Cognitive state anxiety

On page 96, we noted that an explanation for the effect of arousal on a learner's performance relates to the extent of cognitive activity necessary for performance of a new skill. Cognitive anxiety includes fear of failure, difficulties in attention and concentration, faulty decision making and worries about performance. Ziegler (1978) describes how increases in arousal or in cognitive anxiety can create a negative cycle: for example, as performers *perceive* the increase in arousal, this increases their cognitive anxiety, which increases performance errors, which in turn lead to more anxiety, leading to higher arousal, leading to perception of high arousal and therefore more worry and so on.

Sports psychologist Robert Nideffer (1976b) has studied the role of attention and concentration in sport (see p. 161, for more details). He argues that increased arousal causes changes in attention and concentration which can affect performance. In particular, increased arousal may:

- cause narrowing of the performer's attentional field;
- lead to the athlete scanning the attentional field less often;
- cause players to use their dominant attentional style rather than several attentional styles as the occasion demands;
- cause athletes to attend to the wrong cues.

The differing effects of somatic and cognitive state anxiety on performance have been the focus of more recent research. An example is a study of swimmers conducted by Burton (1988). Results show that somatic state anxiety had the predicted relationship to performance – optimal performance was when it was at a moderate level. However, Burton found the lower the cognitive state anxiety the better the performance. A graph showing these results is given in Figure 4.7. This result shows that there is an *inverted-U relationship* between somatic state anxiety and performance, but a *negative linear relationship* between cognitive state anxiety and performance (in other words, the greater the cognitive state anxiety the worse the performance).

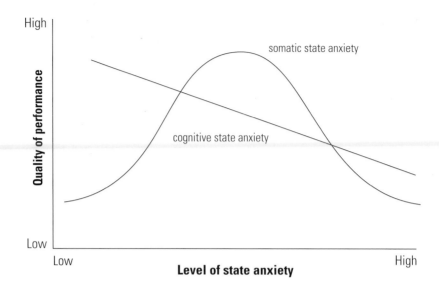

FIGURE 4.7 *Graph showing the relationship between performance, cognitive and somatic state anxiety*

Martens, Vealey and Burton (1990) are amongst psychologists arguing for this multidimensional view of anxiety. They propose that anxiety has three components:

- **cognitive state anxiety**: worry, negative thoughts about performance, fear of failure, disrupted attention, inability to concentrate;
- **somatic state anxiety**: perception of bodily symptoms of anxiety (sweating palms, butterflies);
- **self-confidence**: expectations of success or failure.

Martens and his colleagues (1990) developed a self-report questionnaire to measure anxiety in a competitive situation by assessing each of these three components. This is the Competitive State Anxiety Inventory (CSAI-2), an extract from which is shown in Figure 4.8. Questions relate to the participant's somatic anxiety level (q.8), cognitive anxiety level (q.22), and self-confidence (q.27). In order to measure state anxiety, athletes are asked how they feel at a particular time. Questionnaires may be given to an athlete a week before a major competition, then again 24 hours before, then again 30 minutes before. This helps the coach to find out:

- the 'baseline' level of anxiety and the level of anxiety immediately before competition, to see how they differ;

Competitive State Anxiety Inventory-2 (CSAI-2)

Directions: a number of statements which athletes have used to describe their feelings before competition are given below. Read each statement and then circle the appropriate number to the right of the statement to indicate how you feel right now – at this moment. There are no right or wrong answers. Do not spend too much time on any one statement, but choose the answer which describes your feelings right now.

	Not at all	Somewhat	Moderately so	Very much so
1 I am concerned about this competition	1	2	3	4
2 I feel nervous	1	2	3	4
3 I feel at ease	1	2	3	4
4 I have self-doubts	1	2	3	4
5 I feel jittery	1	2	3	4
6 I feel comfortable	1	2	3	4
7 I am concerned that I may not do so well in this competition as I could	1	2	3	4
8 My body feels tense	1	2	3	4
9 I feel self-confident	1	2	3	4
10 I am concerned about losing	1	2	3	4
11 I feel tense in my stomach	1	2	3	4
12 I feel secure	1	2	3	4
13 I am concerned about choking under pressure	1	2	3	4
14 My body feels relaxed	1	2	3	4
15 I'm confident I can meet the challenge	1	2	3	4
16 I'm concerned about performing poorly	1	2	3	4
17 My heart is racing	1	2	3	4
18 I'm confident about performing well	1	2	3	4
19 I'm concerned about reaching my goal	1	2	3	4
20 I feel my stomach sinking	1	2	3	4
21 I feel mentally relaxed	1	2	3	4
22 I'm concerned that others will be disappointed with my performance	1	2	3	4
23 My hands are clammy	1	2	3	4
24 I'm confident because I mentally picture myself reaching my goal	1	2	3	4
25 I'm concerned I won't be able to concentrate	1	2	3	4
26 My body feels tight	1	2	3	4
27 I'm confident of coming through under pressure	1	2	3	4

FIGURE 4.8 *An extract from the CSAI-2 questionnaire (from Martens et al., 1990)*

- which aspects of anxiety are more evident at which point in the pre-competition period.

Using the CSAI-2 and several other inventories which measure the multidimensional nature of anxiety, researchers have found that typically:

- **Cognitive state anxiety** increases during the days before competition, and remains high but does not increase just before competition starts. Once performance is under way, cognitive anxiety fluctuates, usually as the likelihood of success or failure changes. Research suggests that high cognitive state anxiety has a major impact on performance. Bird and Horn (1990) found, for example, that mental errors made in women's softball were directly related to high cognitive state anxiety.
- **Somatic state anxiety** tends to be low but rises quickly a few hours before the event and decreases during competition. The difference between these two is shown in Figure 4.9.

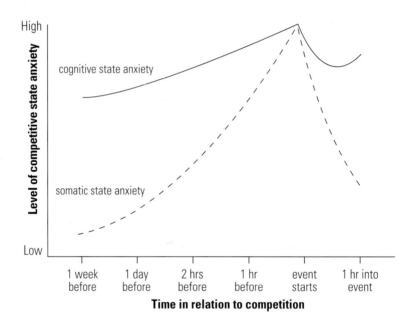

FIGURE 4.9 *Graph showing changes in cognitive and somatic state anxiety in pre-competition period*

Catastrophe theory

Two British sports psychologists (Fazey and Hardy, 1988) noted that performance does not always gradually deteriorate as arousal increases, as shown in the inverted-U hypothesis. Instead, there is sometimes a dramatic decline – a catastrophe in performance. How can both of these outcomes be explained? Fazey and Hardy argue that somatic and cognitive state anxiety do not just have different effects on performance (see Figure 4.7) but that they interact – they have an effect on each other. Fazey and Hardy propose that:

■ the inverted-U relationship applies to a performer with low levels of cognitive state anxiety (one who is not worried); in this case there will be an optimal level of arousal for best performance;

■ increases in cognitive state anxiety will have a *beneficial* effect on performance if the performer is at a low level of physiological arousal;

■ increases in cognitive state anxiety will have a *detrimental* effect on performance at high levels of physiological arousal;

■ if cognitive state anxiety is high then continuing increases in physiological arousal to a high level can cause a large and sudden deterioration in performance – the catastrophe.

■ if a catastrophe does occur, small reductions in arousal will not bring performance back to its previous level; the performer must relax in order to bring arousal below the point at which the catastrophe occurred.

Essentially, Fazey and Hardy contend that physiological arousal has a 'normal' impact but cognitive state anxiety has a 'splitting' effect: it is *cognitive state anxiety* that determines whether changes in performance are gradual or dramatic.

Arousal and anxiety in the elite performer

Research concerned with elite athletes in particular has pointed up individual differences in arousal and anxiety. The work of Yuri Hanin, a Russian sports psychologist, is one example.

RESEARCH
Hanin (1980)

Hanin studied 46 elite female rowers, measuring the levels of state anxiety just before competition and also the quality of the performance. He noted that the mean (or average) level was a score of 43.8, yet individual scores ranged from 26 to 67. This shows how different each individual's level is, so reference to a 'moderate' level of arousal is not useful. This method proved to be time consuming, so he then used a restrospective method which involved asking questions after performance. In this he asked the rowers how they had felt just before their successful performance.

Hanin's results highlighted the individual differences between his participants. Figure 4.10 shows what the arousal–performance relationship might have been for two of them. It can be seen from Figure 4.10 that although each relationship generally shows an inverted-U, the relationships differ, so that, for example, A's optimal performance requires a high level of arousal, whereas B performs best with a low to moderate level of arousal.

As a result of his work, Hanin proposed that each sportsperson has a *zone of optimal functioning* (ZOF), which is the pre-start competitive state anxiety level, plus or minus 4 points. If the level of state anxiety falls within this zone, then the performance will be at its most effective. The job of the coach, then, is to find an individual athlete's zone of optimal functioning, and help him or her to control anxiety levels so they fall within that zone at the appropriate time.

As we see later in this chapter (p. 115), elite performers can tolerate high levels of arousal before they experience a deterioration in performance if they are high in self-confidence. It seems as though self-confidence 'protects' performance, which suggests that developing a performer's self-confidence is vital for success. This relates to Marten's Competitive State Anxiety Inventory (CSAI-2, see p. 103), which includes measures of self-confidence.

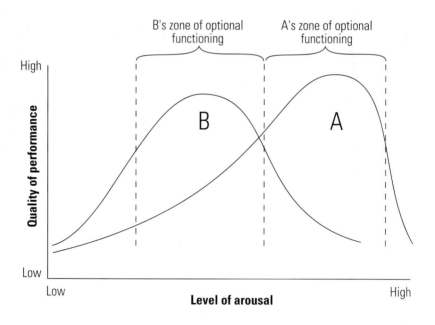

FIGURE 4.10 *Graph showing an imaginary arousal-performance relationship for two participants in the Hanin study*

Measuring arousal and anxiety

We have already come across some of the research into the effects of arousal and anxiety on performance, and have seen examples of three ways in which they can be measured. We will now look at physiological, observational and self-report measures in turn.

Physiological measures

If you read the Weinberg and Hunt (1976) (see p. 101) study of students throwing tennis balls, you will see they used a physiological measure as part of their study. This measures arousal by measuring changes in the body's responses, and physiological measures include:

- monitoring the heart rate – using an electrocardiogram (ECG);
- measuring breathing rate;
- measuring muscle response – using an electromyogram (EMG);
- measuring sweating – the galvanic skin response (GSR) – by attaching electrodes to the skin and connecting them to a voltage meter;
- measuring the level of hormones and steroids in the blood or urine.

Evaluation of the use of physiological measures
There are some difficulties with the use of physiological measures. To begin with, it is cumbersome to 'wire up' the athlete in order to take these measures, which need to be taken before, during and after activity if they are to be of use. Being wired up may increase the athlete's arousal because it interferes with the ability to perform and also affects the athlete's awareness of his or her performance. So the measuring of arousal *itself* may cause increased arousal, thus making results less valid. Testing should occur in a competitive setting in order to study competitive anxiety, but athletes may be reluctant to jeopardise their performance in the name of psychological research. The alternative is an artificial, experimental setting, which may not be an accurate reproduction of the competitive situation (and so lacks external validity).

Some people may show physiological evidence of stress, yet not report feeling stressed. In addition, as we saw earlier, individuals vary in their physiological responses, so that one person may show a rapid increase in heart and respiration rate whereas another may show only an increase in galvanic skin response. It is therefore advisable to use several of these measures to ensure that there is a range of information regarding the physiological condition.

Observation of behaviour

Psychologists have devised observational studies of athletes in which they record how frequently various behaviours associated with arousal occur, and how long they last. The Weinberg and Hunt (1976) study is an example. In order to have a record of the behaviour which can be analysed later by experts, researchers may video behaviour through one-way mirrors so as not to affect the participant's behaviour. Notes will be made of:

- **individual behaviour** such as facial expression, changes in patterns of speech, negative self-talk, fidgetting, licking the lips, rubbing the palms of the hands on clothing;
- **aspects of performance** such as accuracy, speed of reaction.

Evaluation of the use of observations of behaviour

There are a number of difficulties with observational techniques in psychology. One-way mirrors are useful in an experimental setting, such as the tennis ball throwing, but more difficult in the real-world of the athletic track or sports stadium, where filmed behaviour may have to be supplemented with paper and pencil recording. As noted under physiological measures, recording behaviour in this way may in turn increase arousal.

In order to analyse behaviour, there should be at least three specially trained observers so there is less chance of missing something or of one person's bias affecting what is recorded. Training includes learning how to define and assess each of the behaviours being measured so that each observer rates the same behaviour in the same way. For example, when should adjusting your vest be interpreted as fidgetting? Is that athlete frowning or focussing his vision?

Self-report questionnaires

Here, participants are asked how they feel in various situations, using either questionnaires or interviews. Questionnaires are much more popular for both researchers and coaches because they are quicker and cheaper to use. Hanin (1980) used self-report methods in his research on elite female rowers (p. 105).

As we saw earlier under Anxiety (p. 100), two self-report questionnaires are the Sports Competition Anxiety Test (SCAT) and the Competitive State Anxiety Inventory (CSAI-2), which are both examples of Likert scales (see p. 27 for more details). Because athletes complete the questionnaires themselves, they are known as pencil-and-paper self-report measures. Of course, whether you are a coach, teacher or researcher, permission must be given by the athlete to take these measures, and their purpose and what is involved must be explained fully to the athlete before his or her agreement is asked for.

Evaluation of the use of self-report questionnaires

There are some drawbacks with self-report methods. For example, they rely on the honesty of the respondent: there is a tendency to give socially desirable answers rather than completely truthful ones. In addition, the athlete may not recognise the feelings or the labels which the questionnaire contains. For example, if you look at the SCAT on p. 100, what does 'Before I compete I feel uneasy' really mean? When is 'before'? What exactly does 'uneasy' mean? Research suggests these tests may be useful ways of identifying anxiety and self-confidence levels but are not very good *predictors* of an athlete's actual performance.

STRESS

We noted at the start of the chapter that the term stress is widely used to refer to *distress*, the negative psychological and physiological responses which result when the individual feels unable to meet the demands of a situation. Thus, it is the individual's *perception* of the demand which determines whether or not stress will result. A demand which is seen in a positive way ('I'm up for this thanks to all that training. Just let me show them!') will not create stress. We are interested in demands which are interpreted in a negative way and therefore have a *negative* impact on performance. This type of demand is called a *stressor*. Let us take the case of a sprinter who is about to run an important race before a large crowd:

■ demand – the stressor ('This is a major race; what a crowd!');
■ perception of demand ('This is going to be a tough one; that number 7 looks fit');
■ stress response – arousal of the body and anxiety ('My legs are weak; what if I can't hold it all together');
■ outcome – poor performance.

In this section we will look at various stressors, how we perceive or interpret those demands, and finally how we can control the outcome (stress management) in order that damage is minimal and benefit maximal.

Stressors

The demands which are the start of the stress process are called stressors. As sportspeople, we frequently put ourselves in situations which create demands on us. The more threatening we see these demands, the greater the likelihood of arousal and anxiety and therefore, in a sports setting, the greater the likelihood of impaired performance. Some of the stressors which may be perceived as threats are those which:

■ **threaten our self-esteem**: when we are criticised by a coach we may take this as personal and be self-conscious at public criticism; the possibility of losing or being negatively evaluated by others also threatens our self-esteem;
■ **cause personal harm**: for example when going into a game against opponents with a reputation for forceful play, or when asked to try a skill which we feel unable to perform and we fear sustaining an injury;

- **create uncertainty** or **fear of the unknown**: for example when entering a competition, waiting to hear whether we will be selected, sustaining an injury, not understanding what the coach wants;
- **create frustration**: when we are unable to achieve our goals, such as a badminton player whose smash keeps going in the net, a coach who sees her team fall apart against opposition they could easily beat;
- **create pressure**: sometimes the circumstances create pressure (such as taking the penalty shot to win the match) but players can also create pressure. The quotation from Brian Close, England cricket captain in the 1960s, describes the psychological pressure on a batsman which is created by a close fielder:

    'I have only to perch myself at short leg and just stare at some of 'em to get 'em out. They fiddle about and look away and then they look back to see if I'm still staring at 'em. I am. They don't stay long.' (from the *Financial Times* 19.7.97.)

Factors affecting how an individual interprets demands

Whilst all of the above are possible sources of stress, some sportspeople may find them much more stressful than others. It is how we *perceive* the situation which affects our response to it. There are a number of factors which affect our perception of situations:

- **trait anxiety**: as we saw earlier under Trait anxiety (see p. 98), a sportsperson with high trait anxiety has a tendency to see situations as threatening even when they are not. He or she also shows more evidence of stress when in threatening situations.
- **self-confidence**: perception of threat is related to self-confidence. A confident player who has to take a shot at a key point in a match will feel less threatened than a player with low self-confidence, who doubts her ability to take the shot successfully. A confident player will approach unpredictable or unknown situations more positively (and therefore experience less stress) than a player with low self-confidence.
- **individual interpretation of arousal**: if a performer experiences arousal and sees it as positive (a feeling of excitement), then he or she is unlikely to feel threatened. However, if the feeling of arousal is seen as negative, it is likely to be seen as a threat and therefore a stressor. Interpretation of arousal can change very rapidly in a sport setting. Envisage the rugby player kicking a conversion to take the lead: his perception of arousal (apprehension) before the kick will change if he is successful (exhilaration). This is what Schachter and Singer (1962) propose in their cognitive labelling theory. When we are unsure of the reasons for our arousal, we 'label' it according to the circumstances we are in at the time, so athletes

can be encouraged to give an appropriate label to their perceived arousal – one which is helpful to their circumstances.

- **the importance of the event:** the more important the event to the individual, the greater the stress. Lowe's research (cited by Cox, 1994) is an example.

RESEARCH
Lowe (1973)

Lowe studied young baseball players in the USA. He recorded their heart rate when they went in to bat and observed their behaviour, their nervous mannerisms for example. He also noted how important batting was at that time, for example at the end of a close scoring game, or how crucial the game was in the season standings. He found that the more critical the situation, the more tense and nervous the youngsters were.

However, we need to remember that it is how important the event is to the *individual* which matters. A youngster who is selected to play her first netball game for her school in a friendly match against a neighbouring school is likely to see it as a more stressful experience than her team-mate who has played inter-school netball for two years.

Because athletes and coaches have limited control over the demands, they should therefore try to reduce stress by changing the way in which an individual *perceives* the demands. Some valuable ways to manage stress are considered below.

STRESS MANAGEMENT

We have seen so far that the relationship between arousal and anxiety is complex. In addition the term 'stress' has been used interchangeably with arousal and anxiety – for example, the heading for this section could be 'Anxiety Management'. Nevertheless, here we continue to use the term stress to mean the negative response to a demand. Our concern is how this negative response can be managed.

Weinberg and Gould (1995) suggest that arousal is like an emotional temperature. In order to perform to their best ability, athletes need to know their own emotional temperature. In other words, they need to know the level of arousal which leads to maximum performance. Just as we use a thermostat to raise or lower temperature, so techniques can be used to raise or lower our level of arousal (or emotional temperature). We can increase arousal by 'psyching up' and lower it by 'chilling out'. The role of the coach or teacher is to help athletes to identify and use their correct emotional temperature for a particular situation.

The techniques that are most useful in managing stress can be classed as mainly somatic (relating to the body) or cognitive (relating to the mind). It is better to use physical relaxation techniques for somatic anxiety and mental techniques for cognitive anxiety. However, as we have seen, frequently sports-people experience both kinds of anxiety at the same time, so the two types of techniques are frequently used together.

Somatic techniques

The purpose behind somatic techniques of stress management is to reduce the physiological responses associated with arousal.

Biofeedback

In biofeedback athletes use physiological measuring equipment to help them learn how to control their physiological responses. For example, when athletes can hear their heartbeat, they can try to think of something calming in order to find out which thoughts lead to a slowing down of the heart rate. With practice, they will be able to use these thoughts, and heart rate (and arousal) should decrease.

Other measures which can be used are:

- thermometer attached to a finger: because high arousal causes less blood to go to the fingers, they become cold. The athlete watches the thermometer as he tries to control his or her responses;
- electromyogram to measure muscular tension: the measures taken by the electromyogram can be shown on a meter which, for example, makes a loud sound when muscle tension is high. The athlete tries to reduce the sound level by reducing muscle tension. This can be done using some of the techniques mentioned below, such as thinking about being relaxed, perhaps by floating in warm water.

Breathing

Increase in breathing rate is a result of increased arousal, so techniques to reduce it should help bring arousal under control. Because we can slow down breathing by taking deep slow breaths, breathing is one of the easiest ways of bringing arousal under control, when compared to pulse rate or sweating for example.

Muscle tension is released by breathing out, so athletes need first to take deep breaths but they also need to breathe out at the appropriate time in their performance. For example, a gymnast should take a deep breath and let the air out slowly and thoroughly immediately before starting a routine. Taking in and holding the breath causes muscle tension and is therefore damaging to performance.

There are additional advantages to using breathing control as a stress-reduction technique. Not only does it:

- reduce arousal level;
- reduce muscle tension;

but it also:

- helps you to focus so that irrelevant cues are less likely to create distraction;
- is very quick and simple, so can be used in almost all sports situations, whether training, injury rehabilitation or competition;
- provides a brief break from the pressure of the situation, so it helps you gather your thoughts and energies.

The value of breathing is endorsed by Mary Nevill, captain of the British hockey team in the 1992 Olympics, as can be seen from the quotation in the next section.

Relaxation

Somatic anxiety causes muscle tension, but because it is not possible to be relaxed and tense at the same time, the development of relaxation techniques can reduce tension. One widely used method of physical relaxation is progressive muscular relaxation (PMR). This involves tensing and then relaxing groups of muscles in turn over the whole body. Athletes often devise their own techniques along these lines, and practice usually enables the athlete to relax effectively in a very short period of time. Mary Nevill reports that she:

> 'relaxes her shoulders by 'just dropping them' and taking a deep breath. She tries to relax before stick-stopping a penalty corner: "it would just be a moment to physically relax, and... a quiet moment to prepare myself"' (from Jones and Hardy, 1990, p. 263).

Other types of relaxation, such as meditation or hypnotism, involve both physical and mental aspects. Meditation usually involves control of breathing and techniques to help the mind become clear of thoughts by focussing attention on a word or sound, perhaps by repeating a special word (called a mantra). This should take place in a quiet environment.

Hypnosis is not used frequently and, because its effects are not fully understood, it should only be practised by trained professionals. Once hypnotised, the individual is in a relaxed state and can be given suggestions such as 'when you prepare to receive serve you will feel relaxed and confident'. You can see that these suggestions are aimed at reducing both *somatic* and *cognitive* anxiety.

113

Cognitive techniques

These techniques emphasise the role of the mind in managing stress. Several of them are discussed in detail in Chapter 6, Maintaining Participation and Improving Performance, but a brief summary is given below.

Goal setting

Goal setting can help the athlete focus away from the source of stress and on to something achievable. It should focus on performance-related goals rather than on outcome-related goals. Outcome-related goals, such as winning a match, are greater sources of stress because the player has low control over them. An athlete with high levels of competitive anxiety should not set goals which are ambitious or long term because these would only create more anxiety.

Players can be helped to focus on a particular, achievable, goal during performance which can switch attention from the external factors which may create arousal and worry. Consider, for example, a badminton player whose opponent is threatening his serve. If the server sets a goal of serving the shuttle so it skims the top of the net, then his attention is focussed on the shuttle and the net, and there is less attention available to think about what his opponent is doing. For more on goal setting, see p. 154.

Imagery

Imagery is often used with the relaxation techniques noted above in order to reduce arousal. The athlete imagines the circumstances and feelings associated with being relaxed. David Hemery (1986) has described his loss of self-control on the warm-up track when he saw his main rival practising. He felt his throat tighten, the first stage of inner panic. He used imagery to regain control:

> 'I left my shoes off and taking easy strides...took myself back to where I was running in a few inches of water on the firm sands of Powder Point Beach...the sun was on my back and I felt the sensation of my body flowing with health and strength. The image was so strong that my mind was totally blank as to what I had just seen and I was back on to personal performance.' (p.118)

Imagery can also be used to practise (or rehearse) something, when it is known as mental rehearsal or mental practice. An athlete can 'run through' his performance in his mind, deciding how to cope with an opponent's tactics, what shots he will play. By doing this, he is working on some of the possible sources of stress – uncertainty, pressure, low self-confidence – to minimise their effect. He can also run through the situations which are potentially stressful without experiencing the negative outcome. For more on imagery, see p. 157.

Self-talk

The ability to perceive arousal as positive and to maintain a problem-focused attitude before and during performance has a positive effect on performance. Self-talk helps the athlete to see arousal as positive. For example, a sprinter can interpret the arousal she experiences at the start of a race as evidence that 'I'm ready'. Self-talk can be used in other ways, such as to change your perspective of the situation. When Rod Laver, four times Wimbledon singles champion in the 1960's, was becoming very anxious in a match he said to himself:

> 'What is the absolutely worst thing that can happen – I can lose a bloody tennis match' (Hemery, 1986).

For more on self-talk, see p. 164.

Self-confidence

Research shows that self-confidence is closely related to performance. Certainly, the vast majority of elite performers cite self-confidence as a major feature of their success. It seems to protect the sportsperson from the effects of arousal – they see arousal as positive not negative. For example, research with swimmers, cricketers and gymnasts suggests that higher levels of confidence are related to positive perceptions of arousal. Athletes gain self-confidence from previous success and from the knowledge that they can control their perception of the situation so that it is positive. It also comes when the athlete feels mentally and physically ready to perform. For more on self-efficacy and self-confidence, see p. 165.

Stress management programmes

Several stress management programmes have been devised and used successfully in sports settings. They are generally based on the use of one or more of the techniques we have already looked at. Two which have been used in a sports setting are:

- Smith's (1980) cognitive–affective stress management training (which uses PMR and cognitive coping skills);
- Suinn's (1983) visuo-motor behaviour rehearsal (which uses PMR and imagery).

However, recent trends are to encourage athletes to develop these skills themselves, so that they can tailor strategies to their own needs and the particular task they have to perform.

APPLICATION
The role of the coach in reducing arousal, anxiety and stress

The coach can help players by:

- making the demands less threatening, such as by eliminating uncertainty as much as possible, reducing the importance of an event or having players focus on performance-related goals;

- building and maintaining self-confidence by encouraging players to develop a sense of control, such as helping players to learn and apply somatic and cognitive anxiety management techniques, ensuring that they feel they are physically and mentally prepared;

- helping players to change their perceptions, such as putting failures in a positive light – as building blocks for development – by re-casting their self-talk to stop negative thoughts and start positive ones;

- being aware of personal and situational factors, asking what a particular situation means for that player at that time, discovering what is his or her optimal arousal level (the zone of optimal functioning).

CHAPTER SUMMARY

Despite looking at arousal, anxiety and stress as separate topics, this chapter shows that they are closely related. Essentially, there are two components, the physical and the psychological, and it is the psychological or cognitive aspect of arousal that can have the most damaging effect on performance. Nevertheless, individuals differ in their basic anxiety levels (trait anxiety), just as they differ in their response to demands. The key factor is how the individual perceives the demand, and knowledge of cognitive techniques can help alter or modify negative perceptions and consequently improve performance.

chapter five

THE SPORTSPERSON AND OTHERS

CHAPTER OVERVIEW

Most sports activities take place in a social setting, whether training with team-mates, competing in front of spectators, or playing socially in a sports hall. It is because of these other people that we learn skills, become so nervous that we perform badly, can become more aggressive or can be lifted to a great performance through 'team spirit'. This chapter looks at the impact other people have on our attitudes, behaviour and performance.

SOCIALISATION

Socialisation is the process by which we learn the norms and values of our society. Through this process a child's wide range of potential behaviours and attitudes is shaped to fit with what is acceptable in its own culture. In infancy, the socialisation process is dominated by the parent or parents (the primary agents of socialisation). As children's social experiences expand to include school, hobbies, sports, they come in contact with many other influences, known as secondary agents of socialisation. Children's cognitive abilities are also expanding as they start to understand and use language, to make connections between events and to understand abstract concepts such as rules.

Socialisation and social learning theory

Social learning theory provides an important explanation for how socialisation takes place. As a result of his research, Albert Bandura (1977a) proposed that we learn by observing others and modelling their behaviour, which is called observational learning (see p. 69 for more details). The people most likely to be modelled are known as significant others. These are people who are similar to us, who are nurturing or powerful and who are seen to be rewarded for their behaviour. The sports hero is an example of someone who is likely to be used as a model, not just for what he or she does in a sports setting. Butt (1987) notes that:

'The athlete contributes more to the audience than an enactment of competition. He also contributes his way of life. Whatever the admired athlete does, the crowd, particularly the young, tend to emulate.' (p.257)

Social learning theory explains that other people also provide reinforcement. When an individual copies behaviour he or she has seen and the experience is rewarding, the individual is more likely to repeat the behaviour. For example, if a youngster on the field copies the aggressive play of his soccer hero, and his father encourages him from the sidelines, he is more likely to continue to play aggressively. In contrast, if the child's father shows his dislike (punishment) of the aggressive play, then the child is less likely to continue in this way when his father is present. However, if the coach shows approval, the child may play more aggressively when his father is absent. Bandura explains that we learn *when* to show particular behaviours by the consequences that these behaviours bring in different settings.

Sport as a socialising agent

Sport provides the opportunity to observe others and to receive reinforcement and punishment for particular behaviours. It is also an environment in which the values of society are made explicit to the individual. Below are some of the examples of what the child learns through socialisation and how sport may contribute to the process. Children learn:

- what is acceptable, what is important and what is valued, such as success, co-operation, competition, pleasing others, acquiring skills;
- how people behave towards each other;
- how to be accepted by others;
- what is expected of people according to their age, gender, background, body size, culture and so on;
- how to acquire and develop many kinds of skills;
- how to manage their own needs when interacting with others;
- that different social settings require different behaviours.

GROUPS AND SPORTS PERFORMANCE

Groups are important to us; we belong to groups such as our family, and if we play a team sport or belong to a sports club, we are also part of that group. It is through our interactions in the group that we satisfy our need for security, acceptance and belonging. We also learn what is expected and how to behave – we learn group norms.

FIGURE 5.1 *Through sport these players have learned skills, the values of their society, how to co-operate with others and how to satisfy their own needs*

Defining a group

A collection of individuals is not necessarily a group. To be a group there are a number of defining features, namely, there should be:

■ interaction between the members;
■ feelings of interpersonal attraction between members – they should have some positive feelings towards each other;
■ a collective identity in which members view themselves as a unit, distinctive from other groups: this may include the assumption of particular values or ways of behaving;
■ a sense of shared purpose or objectives, which in sports are usually related to group objectives and individual objectives: group members need to interact and depend on each other in order to achieve objectives.

In a sports setting, the group may be a hockey team, an athletics club, a group of climbers or a national sports association. In other words, it may be a team, clearly defined with members having positions and roles to play, or it may be an informal group. However, the word team is sometimes used to denote a very strong group.

Group structure

Every group has a structure: there are members who take on certain roles, either formally or informally. A role is the set of behaviours expected of a person in a certain position. Formal roles are those which are part of the structure of a group, for example a netball team has a wing-attack and a goal-keeper. Players take on a role by performing the behaviours expected of that role, so the wing-attack has different responsibilities, needs different skills, and relates to other members of the team in a different way from the goal-keeper. Apart from roles related to specific positions within a team, there are other common formal roles in sport, such as captain or coach.

Informal roles are those which are not part of the structure but which help the group function. For example, someone who is good at soothing conflict and bringing people together may act as mediator; a player who has been in a team for a long period may take on a 'mentor' role towards new members. Not all roles make a positive contribution to the group; there may be a trouble-maker who engenders conflict or a member with a strong personality who gathers a group of 'followers' and forms a powerful subgroup or clique. However, other members of the group know who plays these roles, and one of the tasks of new members is to find out who performs the unofficial roles.

A team should be more effective if players know what their role is and accept the role. When each players know who is responsible for what, they can see how each of them fits into the team picture and have an appreciation of the tasks of others, as well as of themselves. In addition, a player who accepts his or her role will be more committed and put in more effort. Lack of role acceptance can lead to poorer performance.

How do groups form?

In order to develop fully, a group goes through four stages, as defined by Tuckman (1965):

1 **forming**: initially, team members get to know each other, work out whether they feel they belong to the group and what part they will play. This is the stage when players start to test their relationships with others in the group.
2 **storming**: this stage occurs when conflict develops between members and, in particular, rebellion against the leader; members are jockeying to establish their roles and status.
3 **norming**: co-operation starts to replace conflict; members start working towards common goals. Group cohesion develops, which affects individual satisfaction within the group and may also improve the success of the group. There is increasing mutual respect for each member's individual contribution.

4 **performing**: this stage is achieved when roles and relationships have sta-
bilised and the primary goal for each member is group success.

Group cohesion: what keeps a group together?

We tend to see a group in a positive light if we belong to it, but in a negative
light if we do not. This is the proposal in Tajfel's (1978) social identity theory,
in which he argues that we are biased in this way in order to maintain high
self-esteem. According to this view, then, once we belong to a team or club
we want to stick together and protect our group's interests.

As we have just seen above, however, it is not usually so straightforward. One
of the defining features of a group is that its members have common beliefs,
usually unspoken, about what is acceptable or unacceptable, how things are
done, and so on: these are the *group norms*. As the group develops through the
stages just described, group norms develop. Each member shows his or her
commitment to the group by conforming to these norms. Those who challenge the norms also challenge the group's solidarity, hence groups exert
pressure on their members to conform to the norms. The leader or leaders of
a group have a particular responsibility here: part of their role is to set, maintain and enforce group norms. Such norms may include dress, attitude to
training, treatment of new members and post-match behaviour (Figure 5.2).

FIGURE 5.2 *This team's norm for celebrating success will increase group cohesion*

Some groups are tightly knit, others do not seem to be a 'unit'. It is this internal dynamic, the solidarity or cohesion of the group, which determines how strongly it holds together. Athletes report that team cohesion is a source of satisfaction in their lives, yet there is conflicting evidence as to whether the most cohesive teams are the most successful. This is related to the way in which group cohesion has been analysed – namely, that there are two aspects of group cohesion:

- **task cohesion**: the degree to which group members work together and are committed to achieve common goals, such as winning a match;
- **social cohesion**: the degree to which group members like each other and get on well, trust and support each other.

These two aspects, or dimensions, are independent of each other. In other words, you might be very committed to achieving the goals of your team, but not particularly attached to the other members of the team. A team in which members get on well and are very committed to achieving common goals (they are at the *performing* stage of group development) may be success-ful, but equally a team in which there are major disputes (which could be at the *storming* stage) could do as well if there is a high commitment to the common goal. A definition of cohesion which incorporates these ideas has been proposed by Carron (1982) and is:

> 'a dynamic process which is reflected in the tendency for a group to stick together and remain united in the pursuit of its goals and objec-tives' (from Weinberg and Gould, (1995) p. 183)

Factors associated with group cohesion

The following factors seem to be associated with group cohesion:

- **type of sport**: the cohesive team (in which team members rely on each other to perform successfully) in interactive sports such as soccer tends to perform better, although this is not always true in sports which are co-active (in which individual performance does not depend on others) such as swimming. Here, the degree of cohesion seems to have little effect on performance;
- **stability** in the members of the group: greater stability allows time for relationships between members to develop;
- **the size of the group**: the smaller the group the greater the cohesion, per-haps because there is more opportunity for members to interact and less chance for faulty group processes to occur (see next section);
- **external** threats: these may increase group cohesion by forcing members to ignore internal divisions;
- **similarity** in the status and characteristics of members (e.g. age, skill level);

- **satisfaction** with other team members: greater satisfaction is generally associated with better performance;
- **success** as a group or team: successful performance is associated with greater group cohesion.

Although these factors are associated with group cohesion, the nature of this association is not at all clear because, although successful performance leads to greater group cohesion, providing feedback about group cohesion also improves performance. So does satisfaction with team members lead to success as a team which in turn increases group cohesion, or is it successful performance which increases team cohesion? Psychologists have tried to tease apart the relationships, but with little success to date. It is safe to say that a major reason for the complexity of these relationships is due to their dependence on each other.

APPLICATION
The coach's role in developing team cohesion

Attention to the following points should improve team cohesion:

- Get to know each player and devise ways to help players to get to know each other.
- Encourage open and easy communication between players, emphasising tolerance, listening to others and respecting differences.
- Ensure players know their roles and responsibilities as well as those of others in the team, and the contribution they each make to team success.
- Set challenging but realistic goals which are clearly defined. The goals should be performance based (relating to player's abilities) not outcome based (winning).
- Develop drills and training which develop team (interactive) skills as well as performance skills.

- Value each player and make all players feel they are an important part of the team; minimise the difference in status between roles; encourage players to be involved in team decisions.
- Encourage players to value each other, to support and to give each other positive reinforcement and be constructive rather than critical; discourage the formation of cliques and resolve conflict as soon as it arises.
- Encourage group identity by developing group norms, clarifying group roles, wearing club T-shirts.
- Keep changes to a minimum; encourage group stability.

Factors affecting group performance

A good team is more than a group of skilled players; members need to work together effectively to be successful. Steiner (1972) has proposed that this can be expressed as:

actual productivity = potential productivity − losses due to faulty group processes.

This suggests that in order to improve team performance, coaches need to increase the skills and performance of individual players (potential productivity) whilst reducing faulty group processes. Some of the sources of faulty group processes are competition, poor co-ordination, social loafing and arousal. Let us look at each briefly.

Competition and co-operation

Although competition is an essential part of sporting activity, co-operation is as well, most particularly in team sports. Johnson and Johnson (1985) surveyed numerous studies and found that co-operation produced higher standards in many more situations than did competition, including individual situations. However, most of these studies were not in a sports setting, in which competition can produce exceptional effort as well as damaging consequences. Such consequences may be most evident with younger or novice players, whose experience of failure in a highly competitive setting may lead to withdrawal from the sport. Research shows that females prefer co-operative rather than competitive situations. Increasingly, teachers and coaches are concerned to establish a balance between competition and co-operation in sports.

Canadian sports psychologist Terry Orlick (1978) is one of the main critics of competitive sports, arguing that they have become rigid and evaluative and excessively win orientated. He has developed games which encourage fun, allow the freedom to make mistakes and be sensitive to others' feelings. He proposes that these are also made part of sports and physical education activities.

Co-ordination factors

Another source of faulty group processes relates to co-ordination factors, which are the degree to which each player's skills are meshed together as tightly as possible. This is a particular feature of interactive sports such as soccer, rugby and volleyball. Training time should include practice in passing, timing and the pattern of players' movements. An example is the co-ordination between the three players when taking a penalty corner in hockey, as noted by Horst Wein (1985):

'One notices time and time again that technically superior teams...(can be beaten because of)... lack of concentration, careless positioning and too much improvisation in execution...the penalty corner is grossly neglected in training, especially by club teams.' (p.57)

In contrast, co-active sports such as swimming or golf (where individual performance does not depend on others) suffer less from co-ordination factors.

Social loafing

Social loafing is the term used for the reduced effort that the individual exerts when working with others. It is also known as the Ringelmann effect because in the late nineteenth century Ringelmann measured the amount of effort men put into a tug-of-war task and found the more men were pulling, the less effort each individual put in. In some circumstances, an individual's effort when performing with one other is about 90 per cent of the effort he exerts when performing alone, and with seven others it is about 50 per cent. What are the explanations for this drop in effort? It is seen as resulting from a decrease in motivation, due possibly to:

- the individual thinking the others are not fully committed and not wanting to be the 'sucker': when someone feels that the others are putting in the same amount of effort, motivation increases. Men seem to dislike the 'sucker' role more than women;
- the individual thinking the others will cover up for the lack of effort. However, research shows that when the outcome has personal importance to the individual, he or she will increase their effort regardless of the others;
- the individual thinking his or her efforts will make little difference to the outcome: commitment increases when an individual is convinced that his or her effort will make a difference to the outcome;
- the individual's own effort not being recognised because it cannot be identified in the crowd: effort increases when it is directly monitored and evaluated, as shown by Latané, Harkins and Williams (1980).

RESEARCH
Latané et al. (1980)

These researchers created a simulated swim meet with spectators, trophies and competitors. All swimmers took part in individual and in relay events. Laps were timed; these were announced on some occasions and withheld on others. When lap times were not going to be announced, competitors swam slower in the relay than they did as individuals. However, when times were to be announced, the swimmers were faster in the relay than in the individual events.

APPLICATION
Reducing social loafing

These findings have consequences for coaches. For example, one of the cliches in sports is 'There is no "I" in team'. However, research on social loafing shows that coaches ignore the 'I' at their peril. Group goals are achieved by individuals, so it is important to identify individual behaviours which help group performance and try to encourage those behaviours. Monitoring and feedback on performance (to both individuals and the group) are better than feedback only on group performance. Coaches should therefore monitor individual performance, giving these results as feedback. Monitoring could be done through time checks, videotaping performances, and so on. When providing feedback, it is better to use positive reinforcement (verbal approval and informative evaluations of positive behaviours) rather than rewards such as points.

Arousal

Chapter 4 examines the relationship between motivation and arousal. Maintaining the appropriate level of arousal is therefore a factor in motivating a group. For example, Gill (1986) reports the experience of Emerson (1966) who was a participant observer in a Mount Everest climbing team. His study showed that group members talked optimistically when there were difficulties but talked more about potential problems when things were going well. Essentially, they were maintaining an element of uncertainty, which increases arousal. This is reflected in Zander's (1975) proposal that desire for group success is at its maximum when the group has challenging but realistic goals. This is achieved by operating at a 50 per cent chance of success, which is what the Mount Everest climbers were attempting to maintain. Using this knowledge, how can coaches best prepare their teams?

- Before playing very *superior* opponents, a pre-game talk should be optimistic, stressing the strength of the team, in order to raise self-confidence and reduce arousal.
- Before playing *weak* opponents, the emphasis should be on the strengths of the opposition and things to look out for, in order to raise arousal to an optimal level.

LEADERSHIP

Leadership can be defined as the behaviour of an individual when he or she is directing the activities of a group towards a shared goal (Hemphill and

Coons, 1957). In a sports setting, coaches and captains are leaders, whether of a group, a team or a club. As such, they have an important influence on player satisfaction and individual or group successes. So what makes a good leader? Is there such a thing as a 'born leader'? These are questions which psychologists have tried to answer for quite some time, and we will look at their ideas now.

Are leaders born or made? This question reflects two avenues of research, one of these examines the personal qualities of leaders (the trait approach) and another focusses on the way leaders behave, their *style* of leadership and the situations in which they operate.

The Great Man Theory of leadership: the trait approach

Early this century the emphasis was to identify which personality traits were common to successful leaders. If great leaders had the same characteristics, then this would suggest leadership was innate and that individuals born with these particular traits would be likely to rise to positions of power and influence. It is known as the Great Man Theory. This would mean that a great leader in one sphere (say industry) would also be a good leader in another (sport perhaps.)

There appeared to be some common traits amongst the leaders studied – from business, industry, politics and the military. For example, they tended to be slightly more intelligent, assertive, ambitious and dominant than their followers, but differences did not add up to a clear 'great man' profile and could have been related more to how leaders emerge, rather than how effective they are. So this approach (the *trait* approach) fell into disuse. Instead of studying leaders, researchers looked at what *behaviours* were associated with successful leadership.

Behavioural theories of leadership

This approach views the successful leader as one who displays particular behaviours and proposes that leadership is a skill which can be learned. According to social learning theory, the individual learns leadership by observing others who are leaders then copying their behaviour. If this behaviour is rewarded, then the observer is likely to repeat it, so he or she gradually learns how to be a leader.

For example, a newcomer to a team watches how the captain handles a disagreement between players. When the captain is successful in her efforts the newcomer will remember how the disagreement was handled and is likely to use this approach herself. This is called vicarious reinforcement because seeing someone else being successful after a particular behaviour makes it more likely to be repeated. The newcomer may copy the captain's behaviour when there is disagreement between team-mates and, as she experiences success, will continue to use and develop these skills.

Research on leadership behaviours provided information about leadership styles, the setting in which the leader is working and effective leadership, all of which are reviewed below.

Leadership style

From their research on leadership styles, Lewin, Lippitt and White (1939) identified three different styles of leadership: authoritarian, democratic and laissez-faire. They argued that each style is most effective in particular circumstances, so a leader who can use the appropriate style is likely to be more effective in more situations. The styles are similar to some of the teaching styles described on p. 84, and are described below.

Authoritarian or autocratic style

An authoritarian leader dictates to the group who does what and how, and is most suited when a task must be completed. Advice, ideas or comments are not asked for. Such leaders tend to be rather cool and impersonal and group members tended to be submissive in their attitude to them. Lewin found that when the leader was absent, group members tended to stop or slow down their work and they became aggressive towards each other when things went wrong.

Democratic style

The democratic style of leadership encourages the involvement of the members of the group, ideas are listened to and individuals are encouraged to participate in decisions related to the preparation and execution of group tasks. Nevertheless, the leader takes final decisions and oversees the structure of group work. Lewin found that when the leader was absent, group members continued to work on their tasks and to co-operate when things went wrong.

Laissez-faire style

This style is really 'no-leadership'. Laissez-faire means letting the group members get on with things in their own way. Although leaders may help members get out of difficulties, they offer no direction or involvement, and group goals are less likely to be achieved. Lewin found members of this type of group tended to be aggressive towards each other when things went wrong, and to give up easily.

The interactional approach to leadership

Though valuable, the importance of leadership style is clearly not enough to account for successful leadership. Researchers started to consider additional factors. They distinguished between two categories of leadership behaviour, namely behaviour focussed on:

- **relationships with others**, which requires communication and rapport with others, showing consideration, respect and trust;
- **task achievement**, which requires deciding priorities, identifying weaknesses, creating plans, assigning individuals to tasks and keeping them on task.

FIGURE 5.3 *What qualities does Graham Taylor consider important in an effective leader?*

Graham Taylor comments that:

> 'As a manager you've got to establish relationships with lots of people... they've all got their eyes on you... you've got to be absolutely confident about yourself, even if you turn out to be wrong.'
>
> (From J. Rogan (1989), pp. 257 and 259.)

Research showed that effective leaders were successful at both types of activity. For example, we have seen throughout the topics covered in this book that successful coaches offer encouragement (relationship) at the same time as they provide information to correct errors (task achievement). Effective leadership was seen as depending on other factors such as the particular situation at the time and the type of people who were being 'led'. In other words, an interactional approach developed. We can see what this means for leadership style as we look in more detail at situational factors and members' characteristics.

Situational factors

Fiedler (1967) argued that the effectiveness of a group depends on the personality of the leader and the degree of power the leader has over the situation. Effective leadership therefore depends on (is contingent on) the extent that the individual's style fits the situation. Fiedler's Contingency Model of Leadership argues that leaders have one of two personality traits: they are either relationship orientated or task orientated.

To identify whether a leader was relationship or task orientated, Fiedler measured the leader's attitude to the person he or she found most difficult to work with (called the *least preferred co-worker*, or LPC). Those leaders who saw their least preferred co-worker in a fairly positive way tended to be more tolerant, considerate and *relationship orientated* with group members. Leaders with a very negative attitude to their least preferred co-worker tended to be controlling and dominant in relationships with group members, they were *task orientated*.

Fiedler then went on to describe the types of situations in which each type of leader would be most effective. He argued that:

■ **a task-orientated** leader would be most effective in very favourable or very unfavourable situations. So, if the opposition is very strong, players will understand that tough decisions have to be made and the captain will be forgiven for riding a little roughshod over the feelings of players, because of the pressure of the game.
■ **a relationship-orientated** leader would be most effective in fairly favourable circumstances because the task is more likely to be achieved if everyone is pulling together, so interpersonal relationships are important. For example a captain whose team is playing against fairly weak opposition should keep the players focussed and motivated. Because there is no particular threat, players should be fairly content.

Members' characteristics

To be effective, leaders need to be sensitive to the characteristics of group members, such as their age or skill level. Researchers have studied which leadership style is best suited to a particular characteristic. Some of these are described below:

■ **age**: young players, below the mid-teens, prefer a relationship-orientated approach with low task-oriented behaviours. In general, the research shows that the older the athlete, the greater the preference for a leader who has an autocratic style, emphasises training and instruction but is socially supportive. This suggests that as players get older, they prefer a more controlling style of leader, but this could be because the older players were more skilled. Research into the age of players has generally not distinguished between players' levels of skill, which may have confounded the results.

- **gender**: female athletes prefer a democratic coaching style (which includes participation in decision making), whereas males prefer an autocratic style. Horn and Glenn (1988) found that female athletes who were high in competitive trait anxiety (see p. 99 for details) preferred coaches who provided support and positive feedback. Males' level of trait anxiety appears to be unrelated to a preferred coaching behaviour. Differences in personality characteristics (such as level of self-confidence) between males and females may not be evident before puberty (12–13 years old). Thus, age interacts with gender and personality.
- **ability level**: research is contradictory with regard to ability level, some shows that higher skilled athletes prefer a more relationship-orientated coach, whereas weaker players prefer a task-orientated approach because this focusses on instruction. However, research by Chelladurai and Carron (1983) found that skilled athletes prefer a more authoritarian style. The more advanced athlete is likely to enter more competitive situations, and this, together with possible differences between team and individual athletes, may explain the contradictory findings.
- **personality**: Horn and Glenn (1988) found that athletes with an internal locus of control prefer coaches who excel in training and instruction behaviours, whereas those with an external locus of control prefer an autocratic leadership style. (For more on internal and external locus of control see Chapter 6, Maintaining Participation and Improving Performance, p. 148.)

Effective leadership

How can we measure effective leadership in athletic situations? Chelladurai (1980) proposed that performance outcomes and member satisfaction be taken as indicators of effective leadership. Using an interactional approach, he proposed the Multidimensional Model of Leadership (MML). In this, he argues that certain characteristics generate particular types of leader behaviour. We will identify these first.

Three characteristics

The three sets of characteristics which affect leader behaviour are:

- **situational characteristics** such as whether the opposition is strong or weak;
- **leader characteristics** such as the leader's level of experience, personality, whether goal or relationship orientated;
- **group member characteristics** such as experience, gender or age.

Three types of leader behaviour

The three types of leader behaviour which Chelladurai identifies are:

- **required behaviour**: this is the behaviour required by the situation, such as the type of sport, the goals to be achieved;

- **actual behaviour**: this is what the leader actually does and it is dependent on his or her characteristics, such as experience (see above);
- **preferred behaviour**: this is what the athlete wants the leader to do and it depends on the athlete's own abilities, personality, skill level and so on, as well as the demands of the particular situation.

Chelladurai proposes that if all three of the leader's behaviours are congruent, then member satisfaction and high performance will result. In others words, if the coach does what is required in the situation, and this is what the athletes want the coach to do, this is effective leadership (Figure 5.4).

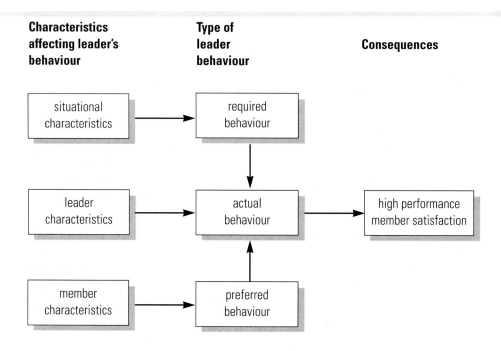

FIGURE 5.4 *Chelladurai's Multidimensional model of leadership*

We can see how this model works by applying it to a specific example. Imagine an under-11 boys' soccer team playing its first match of the season. Many of the boys are new to the club and for a few it is their first experience of competition. How can the coach provide effective leadership? If he looks at Chelladurai's model (Figure 5.4), he can get some answers. The *situational characteristics* do not create pressure to win, so the *required behaviour* is for players to try out their skills and practise working for each other. Members' *characteristics* are youth and inexperience; the *preferred behaviour* from the coach is that he be encouraging and supportive. If the coach's actual behaviour fits these needs, then a high level of performance and satisfaction results. This is effective leadership according to Chelladurai's model.

In contrast, if the same coach is preparing a team of under-16 boys for the final of the inter-regional championships, both the situational and team member characteristics create different required and preferred behaviours from the coach. If his *actual behaviour* does not change then this model predicts that both performance and satisfaction will be low. This model of leadership emphasises the need for flexibility by leaders. From the coach's viewpoint it ties in with teaching issues, where a more effective teacher or coach is one who can employ a range of teaching styles appropriately (see Chapter 3 Learning and Teaching Skills, p. 84).

SOCIAL FACILITATION

If you have been in a situation in which you have performed better when other people were watching, then you have experienced *social facilitation*. Many of us have also had the opposite experience, when skills we can perform adequately suddenly fall apart when we are watched by others. Here, other people cause *impairment* of a task. If our performance improves or deteriorates when others are watching, this is known as the *audience effect*. However, performance may also improve when we are working alongside others. This is called the *co-action effect*.

For the sportsperson, the fact that the presence of others may improve or impair performance is of considerable interest. Explanations for these effects which have been offered by psychologists have been based on research in a non-sports setting. Nevertheless, they have a direct bearing on sports situations. We will review these explanations before considering some specific sports settings.

Zajonc's drive theory of social facilitation

Robert Zajonc's (1965) theory explained how the presence of others could have two types of effects, namely:

- **improved** performance (task enhancement) on a simple task or one which is well learned;
- **damaged** performance (task impairment) on a complex task or one which has not been learned well.

According to drive reduction theory (see p. 68), as a skill becomes well learned it requires less and less drive (or arousal) to be performed. In everyday terms, we could say boredom sets in. Zajonc proposed that the presence of others *increases* our arousal, which in turn increases drive and thus improves our performance of the well-learned task. However, we are likely to make errors on a complex task, so drive theory predicts an increase in drive will lead to an increase in the number of errors when performing a complex task. Critics of this explanation argue that even on well-learned tasks a skilled athlete may perform poorly in front of others. This can be better explained by the inverted-U theory.

Inverted-U theory

As we saw in Chapter 4 (p. 95), the inverted-U theory proposes that arousal affects both physical and cognitive abilities. It enhances performance up to a certain point; beyond that point additional arousal will actually damage performance. The level of arousal that leads to the best performance will vary from athlete to athlete and from situation to situation. For example, when performing a well-learned task, arousal is low but the presence of others pushes it up towards the optimal level, thus improving performance. In contrast, an athlete will already have quite a high level of arousal when performing a complex task or one at which he or she is not proficient. Hence, the additional arousal caused by an audience will push the athlete past his or her optimal level of arousal and thus interfere with the ability to perform the task, so the athlete is likely to make more errors.

Other psychologists have argued that, with humans, we must look at what the presence of other people *means* to the performer. As you will see, the explanations we now turn to take greater account of cognitive factors.

Cottrell's evaluation apprehension theory

Cottrell (1968) argued that it is not the *presence* of others that causes the arousal, but the *apprehension* of being *evaluated* by others – a form of social anxiety. If we are confident about our ability, then the awareness of being watched makes us do the task well. If we are not confident, then whilst trying to do the task we are constantly worrying about how others are evaluating us.

Cottrell showed that the more expert an audience was, the more a performance was impaired. For example, a gymnast who is not completely confident of her routine may perform it well when watched by her family. However, if performing in front of a panel of judges, she is likely to make several mistakes.

Baron's distraction–conflict theory

Baron (1986) incorporated the cognitive approach in his explanation of social facilitation. He noted that we can only attend to a limited amount of information at any one time. We need little attention to perform an easy task but more for a complex one. However, the presence of others demands our attention also, which creates additional and competing demands. It is this conflict that increases arousal and thus leads to either an improvement or impairment of performance. The diagram in Figure 5.5 shows this process.

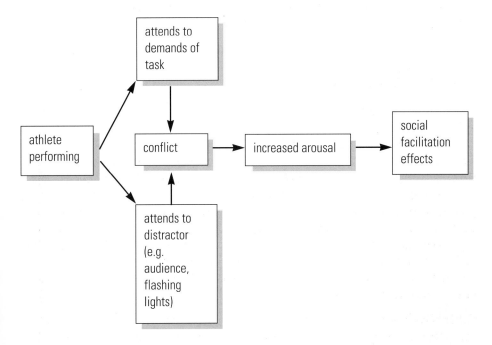

FIGURE 5.5 *Baron's model of distraction-conflict theory*

Baron proposed that *anything* that distracts us will have the same effect, which he demonstrated in a study using flashing lights as a distractor. Results showed that the flashing lights produced the same effect as an audience, namely, that performance on easy tasks was improved and on difficult tasks was impaired. For the sports performer, it suggests that one way of preventing oneself from becoming over-aroused is to direct one's attention to the task in hand and cut out awareness of others.

Social facilitation in a sports setting

Most of the research described so far has studied the effect of an audience when they are passive. However, in a sports setting these others are often active such as supporters. Research on social facilitation in this type of sport setting is limited to date, although one area receiving research attention has been the 'home advantage'. Does playing in front of the home crowd improve or impair performance? Research findings suggest that:

- for the major sports in the USA, teams win more home matches than away matches (between 53 per cent and 64 per cent are home wins). This is true even when the 'away disadvantage' for the visitors, such as the effects of travel and lack of familiarity with the ground, has been taken into account;
- a home advantage may be more important in the early rounds of competition;
- when defending champions are playing at home, there is more chance of the home team cracking under the pressure;
- the home advantage is greater in sports such as basketball, where supports are close to the players. Research shows that it is the intimacy with the crowd, not the size of the crowd, which has most effect.

Earlier we noted another type of social facilitation – the co-action effect. Tripplett (1898) noted that cyclists who were training in pairs cycled faster than those training alone. So performance is improved when others are doing the same task alongside us. This appears to be particularly true when the task is well learned, so for example, players may benefit from training alongside others.

APPLICATION
Using social facilitation in coaching

Research on social facilitation suggests that coaches should keep in mind that:

- sportspeople who train alongside others are likely to put more effort into routine tasks, such as warm-ups;
- when an athlete is learning new skills, it is preferable to keep observers away;
- sportspeople should be encouraged to learn techniques to minimise the effect of distractors, whether other people or noise, heat, and so on. Some of the techniques which help athletes manage arousal, such as relaxation, attention, imagery and self-talk, will be of value. For details, see Chapter 4, Arousal, Anxiety and Stress in Performance, and Chapter 6, Maintaining Participation and Improving Performance.

AGGRESSION

Aggression between players, towards officials and by supporters is a constant source of concern in sport. In several sports (such as boxing or rugby) there are behaviours which would not be tolerated in a non-sport setting, yet coaches may use aggression to 'psych up' their players. Clearly, aggression has an ambiguous role in sport behaviour, so for those who study it one of the first aims is to define just what is meant by aggression.

Definitions of aggression

Gill (1986) proposed that aggression has a number of features:

- it is a **behaviour**: wanting to hit someone is not aggression, but hitting them is, just as *telling* them you are going to hit them is also aggressive;
- it involves **harm** or injury to another living organism: this can be both physical harm (a cracked shin) and psychological harm (creating fear). Smashing a tennis racket is not classed as an aggressive act because it does not involve a living organism;
- it involves **intent**: harm which is done accidentally is not aggression. If a hockey player tackles an opponent on her stick side and catches the stick on her shin, this is an accident.

From this, we could define aggression as behaviour with the intent to harm another. Psychologists have distinguished between two types of aggression, depending on the purpose behind it, namely:

- **hostile aggression**: the purpose of this behaviour is solely to harm someone, headbutting an opponent would fall into this category. This is also called *reactive aggression* and is accompanied by anger;
- **instrumental aggression**: here, aggression is used as a means of achieving a goal, for example tackling hard in order to gain possession of the ball. This is also called *channelled aggression* and is not accompanied by anger.

It is easy enough to differentiate between these two on paper, but in reality it is much more difficult. When a match or competition is in progress, it can be hard to distinguish between hostile and instrumental intentions. Officials have to make immediate decisions about an incident based on what they have just seen, their past experience and, of course, the rules of the game. The rules of a sport define what behaviour is unacceptable or illegal. Some sports researchers have stressed that behaviours which are acceptable in a sport setting are often unacceptable in a non-sports setting. The term bracketed morality is used by Bredemeier and Shields (1986) for the temporary suspension of everyday morality in a sports setting.

This reference to the rules of the game is crucial for clarifying our definitions of aggression in a sport setting. A sportsperson who plays with energy and emotion *and* within the rules of the game is showing *assertive* (not aggressive) behaviours, according to Husman and Silva (1984). Assertive behaviour:

- is **goal directed** to achieve a particular purpose;
- is **not intended** to harm or injure;
- uses only **legitimate force** (even though this amount of force could be called aggression in a non-game setting);
- **does not break** the agreed rules of the sport.

Sports which involve a high level of physical contact such as rugby or ice-hockey are particularly demanding on officials. There is greater opportunity for aggression between players and for discretion on the part of officials who must make decisions. Just as spectators and participants may continue to disagree about an official's decision on an action, so have sports psychologists. However, psychologists tend to use the decisions of the officials in order to distinguish between assertive and aggressive behaviour.

FIGURE 5.6 *It may be difficult for an official to distinguish between assertive and aggressive behaviour*

Causes of aggression

Why are some people more aggressive than others? What effect does the environment have on aggression? Does sport offer an outlet for aggression or create more aggression? You will see there are different answers to these questions as we look at four explanations of aggression.

Instinct theories

Instinct theories view aggression as innate, as an energy which is constantly building up and therefore has to be released. Ethologists argue that aggression is an instinct which has evolved to enable animals to fight for mates, territory or dominance within the group. This fighting instinct creates aggressive energy which must be released in some way, and participation in sport or exploration provides this 'safety valve'.

Sigmund Freud, in his psychoanalytic theory, claimed that we have instincts which have to be satisfied. The instincts create an energy or drive which is used to achieve satisfaction. He claimed that aggression is part of what he called our death instincts, which are destructive. They are in conflict with our life instincts, which are positive and creative. We have to find a way of reducing this aggressive drive by discharging aggression in a way that is positive, such as by exploring, exercising and competitive activities. Just *watching* sport enables aggression to be released – which Freud called catharsis.

Freud also maintained that when we want to do something that we know is not acceptable, we cope by using techniques such as *displacement*. If the boss makes you really angry, you might want to hit him, but you do not. Instead you are very aggressive in your five-a-side match that evening, which is a more acceptable way of releasing aggression. Displacement is an explanation for aggression in sport that is covered later under the frustration/aggression hypothesis.

Critics argue that instinct theories are not good explanations for the causes of aggression because research shows that:

- participation in sport tends to *increase* rather than decrease levels of aggression;
- sportspeople participating in the most aggressive sports should show the lowest levels of aggression outside of their sport, but this does not seem to be the case;
- societies which have a high level of participation in aggressive sports should show low levels of aggression in non-sports settings, but research comparing different cultures (cross-cultural research) does not show this;
- cross-cultural research shows wide variations in the levels of aggression in different societies, which suggests cultural norms are an important influence on aggression levels.

Frustration–aggression hypothesis

The relationship between frustration and aggression has been investigated by a number of psychologists. They take the view that aggression is both innate and learned and that it is related to frustration. Frustration occurs when we are prevented from achieving a goal. In a sports setting this could be when an umpire calls against us, we lose a game or a coach insists that a training schedule continue for another week.

The frustration–aggression hypothesis was proposed by Dollard et al. (1939), who argued that aggression is an innate response which only occurs in frustrating situations. Aggression is *always* caused by frustration and frustration will *always* produce some form of aggression. This view was thought to be too extreme, and it was soon modified by Miller (1941). Miller claimed that frustration makes aggression *more likely*, but for various reasons aggression may not be shown. For example, if a coach insists on continuing a training schedule, the athlete may be frustrated but not show aggression because of respect for the coach and trust in the coach's judgement. Nevertheless, the athlete might shout at her little brother when she gets home. This is related to Freud's notion of displacement. Alternatively, the athlete's response may be to become half-hearted and withdrawn which can lead to learned helplessness (see p. 148).

Frustration causes different responses depending on both the individual and the situation. For example, frustration is *more* likely to produce an aggressive response if:

- the individual is close to achieving a goal (falling in the final lap);
- frustration is caused deliberately (being tripped whilst dribbling the ball);
- the blocking of the goal is arbitrary or unfair (a bad line call).

Berkowitz's aggressive-cue theory

Berkowitz's (1969) aggressive–cue theory introduces *arousal* into the explanation for aggression. He argued that frustration increases arousal, which the individual feels as anger or psychological pain. Most sportspeople are in a state of heightened arousal, particularly when in competitive settings, and therefore frustrations may increase the arousal level to the point where it 'boils over'. This explains why the three circumstances listed above are likely to produce an aggressive response, because participants in any of those situations are already likely to have a high level of arousal.

However, Berkowitz claims that increased arousal does not lead to aggression unless there are cues in the environment. These *cues*, which may be related to aggression or unpleasant experiences, draw out aggressive behaviour. For example, Berkowitz (1969) found that people who had watched the violent boxing film *Champion* were more aggressive than those watching an exciting track race. In another study, he found participants were more aggressive if they had seen weapons (a shotgun and revolver) in a room than if they had seen badminton rackets and shuttlecocks. A diagram illustrating Berkowitz's theory is shown in Figure 5.7.

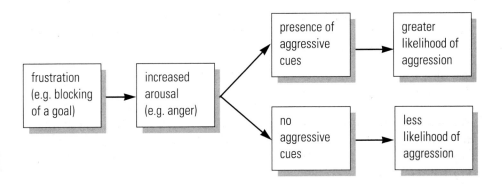

FIGURE 5.7 *Diagram showing the relationship between frustration and aggression (Berkowitz, 1969)*

Sports-related cues which might trigger aggression include:

- objects associated with aggression (guns, boxing gloves, baseball bats);
- sports associated with aggression (boxing, ice-hockey, rugby);
- people associated with aggression (a particular player, coach, fans);
- places associated with aggression (playing on a pitch where there have been aggressive incidents before).

Berkowitz's theory represents an important shift in the thinking about aggression. Whereas the early theories saw it as either as a drive which must come out or at least be an innate response to an external stimulus, Berkowitz emphasised that it was only when there were appropriate environmental cues that aggression would be 'pulled out' of the aroused individual. His theory is therefore linked with the explanations for aggression which come from learning theories (see Chapter 3 for more details).

Social learning theory

According to Bandura's social learning theory, behaviour is learned by observing others. In other words, aggression is not innate; it is learned like any other behaviour. Details of the process of observational learning are given in Chapter 3 on p. 69, and much of Bandura's research on the topic involved studying how aggression was learned. For example, Bandura (1977a) showed that children were more likely to copy behaviour which they saw as appropriate, or which was performed by someone of the same sex, or by someone who was rewarded.

How does this process work? Imagine a young hockey player who sees a team-mate making hard tackles, taking chances and scoring goals. She notices the coach congratulating her team-mate. Seeing her gain rewards (vicarious reinforcement) such as success and approval makes it more likely that the youngster will copy her team-mate's aggressive style. Another example comes from a young soccer player who is watching a match on TV. If he observes a top player arguing and gesturing at the referee, the youngster may copy the model's behaviour in his own matches.

It is clear that the media, particularly TV, is very influential in this process. The way sportspeople are presented, which behaviours are broadcast, sports commentator's attitudes and what is 'newsworthy' shape the viewer's perceptions and, according to social learning theory, their behaviours. In addition, the level of aggression in films or TV programmes appears to be related to levels of aggression in society.

Reducing and controlling aggression

From the material we have just covered we can summarise some of the key factors which are related to aggression:

- the rules of the game;
- the achievement of a goal;
- the level of physical contact in a sport;
- the instinct to be aggressive;
- the presence of aggressive cues;
- the behaviour of others;
- whether aggression brings rewards or punishment;
- arousal;
- self-control.

Every player must take responsibility for his or her own behaviour, but we have seen that a number of factors can make aggression more or less likely to happen. Several of these factors relate to the player's environment, and the coach can help shape that environment and respond to a player's behaviour in a way that could help reduce or control aggression. Several of the techniques described in Chapter 6, Maintaining, Participation and Improving Performance can be of value. Below are some suggestions which make reference to these techniques.

APPLICATION
The coach's role in reducing aggression in sport

- Praise models of non-aggressive behaviour to young players. Remind skilled players that they are role models for others.
- Remove cues which might evoke aggression or remove the player from the situation if possible.
- Provide positive reinforcement when a player controls aggression.
- Teach stress management or relaxation techniques to reduce arousal and control emotions.
- Teach cognitive strategies such as imagery, self-talk or attributional retraining to control aggressive behaviour.
- Reduce the emphasis on winning by decreasing the importance of the event.

- Encourage players to develop performance-related rather than outcome-related goals.
- Emphasise that a player's aggressive behaviour lets the whole team down; support an officials' decision on aggressive play.
- Penalise athletes who persist in their aggressive behaviour.
- As a coach, always be aware of your own behaviour because you can be an influential model. Coaches who permit or encourage players to engage in aggressive behaviour should also be penalised.

CHAPTER SUMMARY

This chapter has considered sport as a social setting through which we learn about ourselves and how to be part of our society. This involves co-operating with others, being part of a group or perhaps leading a group. Others can also improve or damage our performance if we let them! We have seen once again that, despite arguments that our behaviour is largely determined by biological factors such as arousal or aggressive instincts, we can as individuals have some control over our behaviour and the degree to which we are affected by others.

chapter six

CHAPTER OVERVIEW

Sports psychologists have used a number of approaches in their efforts to explain why people continue to participate in sports activities or why they withdraw. In Chapter 1 we looked at the role of traits, such as personality and achievement motivation, which are seen as fairly permanent determinants of behaviour. In this chapter we consider explanations that suggest participation and performance can be influenced. A coach can maintain participation and improve performance if he or she knows the reasons the athletes give for failure, how to maintain their interest and motivate them, how athletes can use their mental abilities to improve performance, and how confidence can be increased. These are the topics we will examine in this chapter.

MAINTAINING PARTICIPATION, AND IMPROVING PERFORMANCE

Gill (1986) has noted the five main reasons why young sportspeople participate in sport: the list is given below. Those who wish to encourage higher levels of participation should ensure that these types of experiences are provided. So far in this book, we have looked at topics that relate to each of these reasons, for example:

- **to learn and improve skills**: Chapters 2 and 3 cover various explanations for how we learn skills, and how skill learning can be made more effective;
- **to get in shape, become stronger, be healthy**: though not mentioned explicitly, these reasons are related to personality, attitudes and self-confidence;
- **to be with friends or make new ones, be part of a group or team**: Chapter 5 in particular looks at how others can affect our behaviour, as well as how groups form and operate;
- **to win, to achieve**: these reasons have been explored in topics such as achievement and motivation (Chapter 1);

- **for excitement, enjoyment of action and challenge**: these reasons have been involved in our examination of personality and motivation in Chapter 1, arousal in Chapter 4 and aggression in Chapter 5.

Nevertheless, there are topics we have not yet covered which are of value to the coach or teacher who wishes to maintain participation or improve performance. These are not two separate aims: the athlete who improves his or her performance is more likely to remain in the sport than the athlete who fails to improve. In this chapter we look at ways in which the teacher or coach can improve performance, which will involve introducing some new material as well as referring back to topics covered earlier in the book. However, the coach needs to remember the reasons why people participate, so we will be mindful that improvements in performance should not be at the expense of enjoyment in participation.

ATTRIBUTIONS

Attributions are the way people explain particular events or behaviours to themselves. These explanations can affect our participation and our future performance. In his autobiography Linford Christie (1995) reports:

> 'After losing at the World Championships in 1991, when I panicked as Carl Lewis came next to me, I decided I had to find some way of concentrating even more intensely so that I could block out everyone else.' (p. 145)

FIGURE 6.1 *Linford Christie beats Carl Lewis at Gateshead in 1992. Perhaps this success was due to the attribution he made for his failure in the 1991 World Championships.*

Here, Christie attributes losing the World Championships to insufficient concentration, which allowed him to panic when he saw Lewis's challenge. Because Christie saw losing as due to something within his control, he felt he could do something about it. Sports psychologists have argued that the reasons we give for success or failure (in other words our *attributions*) can explain a performer's:

- task persistence;
- level of performance;
- expectations;
- satisfaction with performance.

Attribution theory

Attribution theory is an attempt to categorise the attributions people make – whether related to their own behaviour or to what others do. Why did I double fault serve? Did she elbow me on purpose? Is that sprinter too slow off the blocks because he isn't trying or because he didn't understand the coach's instructions?

Bernard Weiner (1972) proposed that achievement is related to the attributions we make. When people were asked why they had succeeded or failed on a task, they tended to give answers which could be classed as due to ability, effort, task difficulty or luck. Weiner argued that these four attributions could be categorised in two ways, or dimensions. They could be either *internal* (like Linford Christie's) or *external* (due to things outside of us). They can also be *stable* (they do not change much) or *unstable* (they may vary widely).

Table 6.1 shows how the four types of attribution are related to the two dimensions. Let us put some flesh on this by imagining a sprinter in Linford Christie's situation – beaten by a strong opponent. He may attribute his failure to one of the following:

- his lack of concentration: this is classed as an *internal* attribution because it relates to the person; as it is also something he could change (he could concentrate more), it is also an *unstable* attribution;
- having less talent than his opponent: this attribution is also *internal* but it is *stable* because talent is fixed;
- the track, where he always does badly: this is an *external* attribution because it relates to the environment; it is also *stable* because he thinks he will always perform poorly on this track;
- traffic conditions which caused him to arrive late and to rush his preparation: this is an *external* but *unstable* attribution – the traffic jam is just bad luck which is unlikely to occur again.

Table 6.1 Four types of attribution

	Internal Attribution	External Attribution
Stable Attribution	lack of talent	an 'unlucky' track
Unstable Attribution	lack of concentration	traffic jam

Weiner stresses that it is not the attribution *itself* which affects behaviour, but how it can be classified within the dimensions shown in Table 6.1. The two attributional dimensions affect behaviour in a variety of ways which have consequences for sports achievement. For example, if our sprinter explains his loss as due to an internal and stable cause (such as insufficient talent), then he will make no effort to change. However, Linford Christie saw the cause as due to something internal and *unstable*, so he was motivated to do something about it. With this is mind, we will look at each dimension in turn, together with the effect on performance.

Internal–external attributions

The internal-external dimension reflects the work of Julian Rotter (1966), who investigated people's beliefs about the extent they feel in personal control of what happens in their lives. Using the term *locus of control*, he proposed that those with an internal locus of control believe that what they do can influence outcomes. In contrast, those with an external locus of control believe that outcomes are influenced by *external* factors, such as luck, fate or other people, over which they have no control.

Rotter (1971) suggests that the ability to make internal attributions indicates greater maturity, suggesting that involvement in sports can help shift attributions from external to internal control. For example, Duke et al. (1977) observed a significant move towards internal control in 6–14 year olds as they reached the end of an eight-week sport fitness camp.

Attributing outcomes to our own efforts can create emotions, such as feelings of pride ('My preparation strategy really paid off') or shame ('I let my coach down badly with that performance'). Internal attributions create more powerful emotions than external ones – pride at winning because of *effort* is more intense than winning because of *luck*. These emotions are an indicator of attributions, according to Weiner. A speedskater who wins a race because she has beaten everyone else will show more exhilaration in her voice and body language than one who has won after the leading skater fell (the predominant emotion here may be gratitude).

Internalising success leads to increased self-confidence, but internalised failure may lead to shame, feelings of incompetence and eventual withdrawal. This is one reason why the coach should take particular note of athletes who hit a bad patch, and ensure that their attributions do not lead to eventual withdrawal.

Stable – unstable attributions

The stability of our attributions is based on past experiences ('In the last five matches we've never beaten them') and therefore creates expectations about the future ('We'll probably lose this match too.') We anticipate the same outcomes if we hold stable attributions. What if, to our surprise, we win the sixth match? We are likely to attribute the cause to an unstable factor such as luck.

This is equally true if our past experience has been of success, but then we fail. We are likely to give an *unstable* attribution, which means we would expect a different outcome next time. The attribution may be external (bad line-calls) or internal like Linford Christie's. Christie's perception of failure was due to insufficient concentration; he could improve his level of concentration and therefore could expect a different outcome next time.

So, the stability of our attributions affects our response to failure. If our attribution is stable, then we cannot change it, so there is no point in trying to do anything. If I am convinced that I am not able to shoot goals, then because my lack of ability is something which cannot be changed, there is no point in practising, concentrating or using any other technique. Of course, I may be wrong! Errors in our attributions are discussed on p. 150.

Controllability and learned helplessness

Before we look at why it is useful to categorise attributions like this, we will consider another dimension which Weiner added in 1979 – controllability. This also relates to Julian Rotter's (1966) locus of control, which he saw as a personality trait and therefore fairly permanent. There has been some debate about how this relates to the other two dimensions, so it less widely used. However, Weiner's point is that controllability is not a trait but one of the ways in which we explain events, whether they relate to our own circumstances or to the circumstances of others. He divided controllability into personal control and external control.

If, for example, we attribute someone's failure to something beyond their control (called external control), we will blame them less and treat them more kindly than if we attribute their failure to a factor within their control (personal control). The coach who is working on the hand-over with a relay team may attribute the third man's weaknesses to his lack of concentration. Because the third man has control over this, the coach's attitude will be more critical than if he sees the athlete's weaknesses as due to the way the second man prepares for the change-over (over which the third man has little control; Figure 6.2).

FIGURE 6.2 *If the receiver makes an error in this change-over the coach will be more critical if he attributes the error to something which is within the athlete's control*

Most of us prefer to feel in control of our own destiny, and not at the mercy of external forces, not controlled or dictated to by others. When our freedom is threatened we react, but if our efforts to regain control continually fail, then *learned helplessness* may result. Seligman (1975) coined this term and, briefly, it means that the individual learns (by the repeated inability to change something) that failure is inevitable, so he or she becomes passive and loses the motive to act: because of my repeated failure to get a netball through the ring, I may eventually give up altogether.

However, people vary in the degree to which they succumb to learned helplessness, depending on their beliefs as to why they are unsuccessful – in other words, depending on their attributions. If I attribute my failure to an *unstable* factor such as poor concentration, then I have reason to keep trying and am unlikely to develop learned helplessness. Some ways of combatting learned helplessness are considered on p. 152.

Errors in attribution

We are, of course, not always accurate in the attributions we make. On the one hand we have a tendency to favour ourselves when we explain outcomes; on the other, our attributions may be based on wrong judgements. We will look at these types of errors below.

The self-serving bias

We tend to be biased in our attributions because we explain behaviour or outcomes in ways which protect our self-esteem. For example, we attribute successes to internal reasons ('We won because our passing was more accurate') and failure to external reasons ('We lost because of poor refereeing'). Gill (1986) notes that teams blame losing on poor refereeing but never claim *success* is due to poor refereeing!

Research in a sports setting shows some interesting variations to this pattern. When Gill (1980) asked women basketball players the reason for their successes and failures, players showed the usual bias – their successes were due to their team and failures were blamed on the other team. However, when they were asked to say whether the result was due to themselves or their team mates, winning team members attributed success to their team-mates and failure to themselves.

This reversal of the tendency to take credit for success and blame failure on others is also evident in the elite athlete. As we saw above, Linford Christie blamed failure on himself. Clearly, the more likely it is the athletes take responsibility for failure, the more likely it is that they will take steps to make changes.

The actor–observer effect

Researchers such as Nisbett et al. (1973) noted that attributions differ depending on whether an individual is the actor or the observer. They proposed that:

■ when the individual is the actor, he or she tends to attribute their behaviour to *external* factors, which are therefore out of the individual's control ('I dropped that catch because the sun was in my eyes');
■ when observing the same behaviour in *others*, the individual attributes the behaviour to *internal* factors, which are *within* the other person's control ('He dropped that catch because he wasn't concentrating'; Figure 6.3).

Incorrect attributions and gender differences

Research outside of a sports setting suggests that males differ from females in their attributions of achievement. Females have lower expectations of success than males in most achievement situations (Lenney, 1977) and females are more likely to attribute success to luck (external and unstable) and failure to lack of ability (internal and stable). In contrast, males tend to attribute success to ability (internal and stable) and failure to external factors.

FIGURE 6.3 *An observer would give a different reason than this fielder for his dropped catch*

Research in a sports setting suggests that these differences are apparent even in youngsters. For example, Bird and Williams (1980) found that 13-year-old males usually explained success as due to effort, whereas females of the same age attributed success to luck. Such findings reinforce results which show females tend to be lower on self-confidence and on levels of participation, particularly in competitive sport.

Attribution and achievement

What are the implications of these dimensions or patterns? Weiner (1972) argues that high and low achievers can be distinguished on the basis of their attributional patterns. Because high achievers attribute their success to internal reasons, and experience pride in their successes, they seek out more opportunities for success. In addition, because they attribute failure to unstable factors, they are more likely to persist after failure because it is possible to change. In contrast, low achievers tend to attribute failure to stable factors and therefore give up, because they think there is little they can do to change things.

Essentially, Weiner's attributional theory of achievement behaviour asserts that motivation and high achievement are due to cognitive factors (the way we think, our understanding of events) not to personality factors (such as Atkinson's achievement motivation, see p. 2). Nevertheless, research in both areas has become closely related.

Attributional retraining

Although attribution theory helps us to explain individual behaviour, it does not tell us how right the individual is! Our losing sprinter may be extraordinarily talented, but if he is convinced that he does not have enough ability, then he is unlikely to try to improve his performance. We have already noted that some attributions may be damaging to the athlete's persistence and level of performance, and may lead to a state of learned helplessness. Here, the coach has a role in helping athletes to develop attributions which will improve their performance; this is known as attributional retraining. Dweck's (1975) research on learned helplessness is a valuable starting point for designing an attributional retraining programmes.

RESEARCH
Dweck (1975)

Dweck worked with children classed as helpless, who saw failure as inevitable (a stable attribution). Half of the children were given easy tasks and therefore only experienced success. The other half also had tasks which they were successful in, but on a few they failed. At this point the researcher encouraged the child to attribute their failure to lack of effort (an unstable attribution). The intention was to recast the children's attributions of failure from stable to unstable. All of the children were subsequently given a range of tasks, and results showed that those who had been encouraged to recast their attributions responded better to failure and performed better overall; those who had experienced only easy tasks showed no improvement.

Dweck's study suggests that in cases of learned helplessness the outcome of the task has little effect on the child's attributions: the coach or teacher must help the child change his or her attributions. The coach's job is to help the player achieve success, and to ensure that success is attributed to stable, internal and controllable factors. Players then see success as within their own control, and approach new challenges with expectations of success. When failure occurs it will be seen as unusual, and thus be labelled unstable. So it is possible to change.

There are a number of strategies for attributional retraining which are listed below.

APPLICATION
Attributional retraining

As a coach or teacher you should:

- observe which situations athletes approach or avoid and how they respond to success and failure; these observations will suggest the type of attributions the athletes are making;
- remember that errors in attributions may be due to the performer, the observer or because of their gender;
- keep in mind that as an observer you may tend (wrongly) to see outcomes as being within the athlete's control;
- encourage the performer to view success as due to stable and internal factors (such as ability); this should encourage pride and confidence in future situations;
- help the performer to view failure as due to unstable factors, both internal (poor concentration) and external (strong competition); this encourages the performer to take responsibility for performance, yet maintain self-esteem by viewing failure as partly outside of his or her control;
- monitor your own feedback because this can help alter attributions: your comment to a young soccer player might be 'You missed because your head wasn't over the ball. Remember... Try it next time; you'll get it with practice.' This attributes the player's failure to poor technique (internal and unstable so he can do something about it!) It then provides information to correct the technique and ends by showing your confidence he can do it if he persists;
- make attribution retraining an ongoing programme: one-off efforts to change attributions are not enough.

REWARDING BEHAVIOUR

At several points throughout this book we have noted that if behaviour is rewarded, it is more likely to be repeated. (For details see Chapter 3 Learning and Teaching Skills.) We can reiterate those points, as they appear to have considerable influence on maintaining participation and improving performance.

Reinforcement and punishment

- **A reinforcer** is anything that strengthens behaviour, or makes it more likely to be repeated. Coaches who say 'nice pass', give a thumbs up or award a medal are aiming to reinforce correct behaviour. Such reinforcement should be given as soon as the behaviour is performed for maximum effectiveness.

■ **Punishment** is anything which weakens behaviour, which would be the intention of a coach who dropped a player for abusing the referee. However, if a training schedule is such that players fail to turn up or perform half-heartedly, it is weakening their behaviour and is classed as punishment. Teachers and coaches can judge their effect on players by noting whether what they do as instructors weakens or strengthens their players' behaviour.

Extrinsic and intrinsic motivation

These two types of motivation are explained in Chapter 1, where you can see that extrinsic motivation is reinforcement which is external to the performer, such as saying 'good try' when a skill is first performed. The 'good try' is seen as rewarding: it motivates the performer to repeat the effort. In contrast, the satisfaction of hitting a tennis ball well comes from inside yourself. Thus, satisfaction is an example of intrinsic motivation. Because extrinsic motivation must be continued once it has been established if performance is to be maintained, and because extrinsic motivation may damage intrinsic motivation, teachers should:

■ use extrinsic motivation generously with novices, and when a new skill is being learned;
■ gradually withdraw extrinsic motivation so that the external rewards are only intermittent;
■ encourage the performer to develop intrinsic motivation in order to become a more independent learner.

GOAL SETTING

Most of us are good at setting goals – New Year's resolutions, losing weight, saving up. We are less successful at achieving those goals, perhaps because they are unrealistic, too vague or take too long to achieve. The sportsperson often sets goals spontaneously, for example to play for a team in the local five-a-side league or to represent his or her country at swimming. These can be seen as long-term goals, and their achievement requires breaking them down into short-term goals, which is what goal setting entails.

Why is goal setting useful?

Goal setting (see Figure 6.4 for an example) is valuable because it:

- helps the performer persist: by making performance measurable and specific over a short time span, the achievement of long-term goals is seen to be not only attainable but as being attained;
- directs attention to a particular skill: this focusses learning and reduces uncertainty;
- motivates the performer: by providing feedback on performance and increasing confidence;
- reduces stress by focussing on a particular goal during performance: by working on this goal the athlete is able to focus attention on it, thus protecting against arousal from other sources and providing self-confidence prior to competition;
- helps in the achievement of long-term goals.

Hit a tennis ball against a wall 12 times, using the goal sequence detailed below. When a goal has been achieved successfully move on to the next:

- Goal 1: 12 strokes – using any groundstrokes
- Goal 2: 12 strokes – including 4 backhands
- Goal 3: 12 strokes – using alternate 1 forehand/1 backhand
- Goal 4: 12 strokes – using alternate 2 forehands/2 backhands

FIGURE 6.4 *An example of goal setting for a novice tennis player*

Types of goals

The type of goal which people set themselves may be classed as having either a performance orientation (also called task or goal orientation) or an outcome (or win) orientation. The *performance orientated* sportsperson focuses on his or her own performance, sets personal goals and aims to improve performance from the previous time – to develop mastery. For example, a tennis player might aim to get 10 out of 12 serves in court throughout a match. Those with a performance orientation are more likely to feel in control, to select realistic tasks and opponents, and are less likely to feel that losing is a major setback – so they are more persistent and do not fear failure.

In contrast, *outcome orientated* athletes judge their success in comparison with others, such as winning a race. Because the outcome of such competition is less within their control, it is more unpredictable, so outcome orientated people have more difficulty maintaining a feeling of competence. Their perception of their own ability depends on the outcome of these comparisons; several failures are likely to make them feel incompetent. To protect their self-worth they may choose to play in situations in which they are bound to win or bound to fail. They are less likely to remain motivated than performance orientated sportspeople. Clearly, coaches should try to foster a performance orientation in their athletes.

Characteristics of good goal setting

In a sports setting, we are not concerned particularly about goals such as feeling fitter, but about the specific *ways* in which such a goal might be achieved. Telling players to try harder or practice the run-up is not very helpful for them because it is too general; it is much better to help them devise a specific target to aim for. This means identifying some clear ways of measuring fitness or identifying particular features of the run-up which can be practised.

To be effective, the goal which is set must take account of the sportsperson's ability, attitude, anxiety level, self-confidence and motivation. For example, a youngster just learning hockey will need to have goals which are easily achievable within a short time-span in order to increase confidence and motivation. In contrast, a well-motivated county hockey player would benefit more from goals which were challenging and may take a while to achieve. In such cases, inappropriate goal setting can damage performance, just as appropriate goal setting can enhance it. In either case the player needs to be involved in setting the goal, because this increases his or her commitment to it. Players must also know when the goal has been achieved, which is why the goal must be specific and measurable. These principles can be used by coaches and athletes using the acronym SCCAMP, as detailed below. To be successful, goals must be:

- **specific**: the athlete needs to know exactly what he or she is working towards, and when it has been achieved. It should also be clear how a particular goal fits into an overall strategy of improving performance.
- **controllable**: goals should be within the athlete's control and not depend on the performance of others. Performance orientated athletes are likely to set goals over which they have control, whereas outcome orientated athletes depend more on the performance of others for achievement of their goals. Athletes should therefore be encouraged to understand the difference between the two and to set performance rather than outcome goals.
- **challenging**: a challenging goal provides incentive and satisfaction when it is achieved. However, the particular needs and abilities of the athlete are crucial in determining what is challenging for him or her. For example, as we saw in Chapter 1, athletes with a high motive to avoid failure may require particular help in setting and achieving goals because they are more likely to set inappropriate goals which ensure either success or failure.
- **attainable**: this relates to the previous point in so far as goals must be realistic so that they are attainable. It is the achievement of the goal which increases performance and motivation. If the initial goal proves difficult to achieve,

then it should be revised so that it is achievable, otherwise the athlete may become disheartened.

■ **measurable**: devise goals which can be easily measured and recorded, (such as performance time), give the athlete accessible and explicit feedback. It is useful if the record is easily visible to the athlete – perhaps in a gym, changing room, or in the athlete's home. Goals which involve lengthy observations are less likely to be recorded and read. Some goals, such as reducing anxiety, may be difficult to measure. Nevertheless, if the athlete completes a self-rating scale such as the CSAI-2 (see p. 103) on a series of occasions it is possible to compare changes over a period of time.

■ **personal**: this means goals should relate to the individual's own needs and abilities and be decided jointly by athlete and coach. This enables the athlete to feel committed to the goals. In the longer term, the coach's aim should be to support athletes in the setting of their own goals. Once set, the coach's role is to provide encouragement and feedback which will help the athlete to persist, as well as monitoring that the goals are indeed appropriate and, if not, to help the athlete reset the goals at a more achievable level.

Our focus has been on goal setting for the individual, but it is valuable for teams as well. However, even the experts sometimes get it wrong. Geoff Cooke coached the England rugby team for the 1991 World Cup. England lost in the final, and he says his biggest mistake was:

> 'I didn't cement the goal of winning firmly enough in the psychological preparation. England was not expected to succeed and I set so much store on reaching the final – once the team had won the semifinal it was their goal achieved!' *National Coach Foundation magazine*

IMAGERY

Athletes who speak of visualisation, mental rehearsal, imagery or mental practice are all referring to the process of creating an experience in the mind – of imagining something. Imagery can be used to experience many aspects of skill learning and sports performance. David Hemery (1986) describes his preparation for the Olympic 400 m hurdles as

> '...apart from the physical practice, many more hours were spent mentally rehearsing the effort distribution, pace judgement, stride pattern and hurdling technique for a successful attempt.' (p.114)

Using the senses

If David Hemery was mentally rehearsing what it felt like to clear a hurdle, he was using his kinaesthetic sense – the sense of the position of the limbs and their movement. So, although we refer to visualisation or imagery, we mean not only what we *see* in our minds but also what we hear and smell, and what we feel in our body. Indeed, using imagery is more effective if it can be made more vivid by involving other senses. For example, David Hemery could create the feel of his foot hitting the ground, the sight of the next hurdle approaching and the sound of his own rhythm of steps in order to make his imagery more intense.

This discussion of the use of all the senses in imagery relates more to *internal* imagery. This has been distinguished from *external* imagery as follows:

- **internal imagery** is imagining yourself doing something, so you experience how it *feels* to do something;
- **external imagery** is seeing yourself do something as though watching yourself on film.

Developing imagery skills

Nideffer (1985) outlines ways of developing imagery skills, noting that some of us seem to use them naturally whereas others have great difficulty in developing them. To develop imagery skills he advises us to:

- decide what we want to mentally rehearse, which aspects we want to focus on;
- practise imagery when we are relaxed, without distraction and not close to performance;
- use internal imagery to practise physical skills, imagine performing the movement, concentrate on tension in the muscles, which parts of the body are moved, the sequence in which movements occur, what we can see as we perform the movement;
- learn to time the mental rehearsal so it takes as long as performing the action in 'real time';
- practise external imagery by looking at ourselves from various angles as we perform the movement;
- learn to use internal and external imagery interchangeably.

Imagery can be used by sportspeople for a variety of purposes. The main uses of imagery are described below.

Mental training, mental rehearsal or mental practice

All three terms are used to refer to the regular and intensive mental practice of an action without physically performing it, just as David Hemery described. The benefits of *mental* training are well-documented. Feltz and Landers (1983) reviewed many studies and found that when mental rehearsal of an action is combined with *physical* rehearsal, this improves performance when compared to physical rehearsal by itself. In particular, mental training is more effective for skills with a large cognitive component, such as those which are just being learned, involving long sequences (such as gymnastics) or those involving decision making and strategies. It has limited effect on skills with a low cognitive aspect, such as those relating to weight-lifting.

Why does mental training have this effect? A number of explanations have been offered. The first four of those listed below are particularly valuable for the novice. Mental training:

- enables the performer to try out different strategies, to correct faults by replaying the skill correctly, to break down the performance of a skill into subroutines;
- allows the sportsperson to perform without risk of public failure;
- avoids the arousal caused by performance in front of others;
- allows the athlete to suspend time and motion: for example, a gymnast can mentally rehearse take-off for a forward roll, can then focus on tucking in the limbs, and can then focus on the landing, taking as much time as is necessary to mentally rehearse each stage; the whole routine can then be mentally rehearsed as one unit;
- activates the sportsperson so he or she is attending to the right cues, is prepared to expect certain stimuli, and is prepared to respond to each of the stimuli. Some researchers, such as Suinn (1980), have proposed that mental training causes slight activation of the neuromuscular system, so it is like a weak form of physical training. This is because research on internal imagery shows that there are tiny muscle movements which reflect the movement of the muscles if they were actually performing the skill. For example, if David Hemery had monitors attached to his leg and arm muscles when he was mentally rehearsing for his 400 m hurdles, the monitors would show tiny muscle movements in his take-off leg as he imagined taking off. This helps athletes to establish the appropriate activation pattern for the skills required so they are less likely to be disrupted if anxiety occurs;
- can be used during injuries to help athletes keep 'on top' of skills they are unable to perform physically.

Imagery and strategies

Imagery allows athletes to work through various strategies, to 'run through' a performance in their mind, perhaps by deciding how to cope with an opponent's tactics, what shots he or she will play, imagining a performance against different opponents or in differing weather conditions. The sportsperson can also run through the situations which are potentially stressful without experiencing a negative outcome. This enables a player to feel prepared and so increases confidence. Chris Evert described how she had visualised what might happen against a particular opponent and played the appropriate shots. She reported:

'I felt I had already played the match before I even walked on the court.'

(Hemery, 1986)

Controlling arousal and emotions

Imagery is often used with the relaxation techniques to reduce arousal (for more details see Chapter 4 Arousal, Anxiety and Stress in Performance, p. 114). The athlete imagines the circumstances and feelings associated with being relaxed, often in combination with other techniques such as deep breathing, and becomes better able to cope with arousal or stress.

Arousal and emotions are closely related. Jackie Stewart described how he used imagery prior to a Grand Prix race. He saw his emotional state as 'an over-inflated beach ball': during his emotional countdown towards the race time he would gradually deflate the ball until it was completely deflated and he was virtually emotionless. Daley Thompson recounted how he psyched himself up prior to performance and at the same time prepared himself for extreme pressure. He reported:

'I imagine myself standing on the high jump area having had two failures and the bar is at 2 m 10 cm, so I've been there before.'

(Hemery, 1986, p. 117)

Although the above quotations are what we call anecdotal evidence, research which provides experimental evidence has confirmed that approximately 90 per cent of elite athletes use some kind of imagery, and attest to its value, although the reasons why it works are less clear. Research suggests that:

- tasks requiring mostly cognitive components, such as decision making and perception, show the greatest benefits from imagery rehearsal (Feltz and Landers, 1983). Such rehearsal enables the athlete to think about a number of options and what the consequences might be;
- imagery seems to enhance the performance of experienced performers more than of novice performers. It seems to help them refine skills and to make decisions or adjustments very rapidly;
- imagery may help novice performers learn cognitive elements relevant to successful performance of a skill, such as by modelling the performance of the skill by an experienced player.

ATTENTION

John Newcombe describes his 1969 Wimbledon final against Ken Rosewall like this:

'after one set all ... suddenly it was 6–3 to him (in the third set) ... I had just 60 seconds changing ends to get my act into gear ... I just said to myself ... you'd better put yourself into some sort of zone where you just see Rosewall and the tennis ball. Within that 60 seconds I put myself into a cocoon ... I played the fifth set and beat him 6–1, everything he did, I knew he was going to do it before he did it.' (Hemery, 1986, p.251).

Concentration is focussing your attention on the relevant cues in the environment and keeping that focus. You can see from the quote above that Newcombe decided the relevant cues were Rosewall and the ball. By keeping his *attentional focus* on those cues, he was able to play in the 'flow zone'.

Attentional focus

The kind of attentional focus used by Newcombe would be a handicap to a basketball player. Different settings require different types of attentional focus. Sports psychologist Robert Nideffer (1976b) proposed that attentional focus has two dimensions:

- **broad or narrow**: when it is broad the player can see several things at the same time, such as the positions of key players when a ball is being dribbled up the field. When it is narrow the player is focussing on only one or two cues, such as John Newcombe focussing on Rosewall striking the ball;
- **external or internal**: external attentional focus is directed outwards towards, for example, the bounce of the ball or the position of a player. Internal attentional focus is directed towards the individual's own thoughts or feelings.

These two dimensions can be combined to give four different types of attentional focus. These are shown, together with examples, in Table 6.2.

Table 6.2 Four different types of attentional focus

	External	Internal
Broad	Broad-external (e.g. used to check positions of other players	Broad-internal (e.g. used to plan tactics or strategy
Narrow	Narrow-external (e.g. used to watch racket strike ball)	Narrow-internal (e.g. used to control anxiety)

Attention, arousal and performance

Nideffer (1976a) introduced the notion of overload, which occurs when we have too much information to attend to at one time. For example, a hockey player who misses a crucial goal may think of how she has let her team down, may hear the opposition supporters' cheers of delight, and may be thinking of what she did wrong and how the match can be retrieved. All this mental activity may lead to *cognitive overload*, so that if someone makes a tactical suggestion or comment on the game she does not even hear it. Nideffer argues that increased arousal causes changes in attention and concentration. These can affect performance by:

- causing the athlete to scan the field less often so that a player can take her by surprise, or she fails to take in the full pattern of play so that she misses opportunities to spot weaknesses or to score;
- causing the athlete to attend to the wrong cues, so she may start to think about her footwork or notice the crowd's behaviour and thus performance deteriorates;
- making the athlete fall back on her dominant attentional style (see the next section for more details): to be effective, many sportspeople need to be able to use several attentional styles as the occasion demands;
- causing narrowing of the performer's attentional field: this is a handicap for rugby players, who need to be aware of all that is happening around them (Figure 6.5), but advantageous to the gymnast because a narrow attentional field enables them to shut out distractions and so focus on the move they are performing.

FIGURE 6.5 *This rugby player needs a broad–external attentional focus to make an effective pass*

Attentional style

Nideffer (1976b) has argued that people have different attentional styles, which means that they have a natural tendency to use a particular style. He classified people as *effective attenders* or *ineffective attenders*. Let us look at the abilities of the two types.

- **Effective attenders** do not become overloaded. They can deal simultaneously with several aspects of information which come from outside themselves (the cheers of opposition supporters) and from inside themselves (thoughts of what went wrong, how they let the team down). They can also switch from a broad-external to a broad-internal focus very quickly, and can narrow their focus of attention without missing any important information.
- **Ineffective attenders** do not concentrate well and tend to become overloaded and confused. They have trouble narrowing their attention effectively – so, for example, they may be unable to block out the shouts of the opposition supporters – or they may narrow their attention so much that they fail to notice something important such as the position of another player.

Clearly, the sportsperson who is an effective attender has a great advantage, and those who are ineffective attenders will need help to switch their attention from broad to narrow when necessary, and perhaps help in stress reduction in order to reduce arousal. In addition, the demands of particular positions on the field require different types of attention, so a player may perform better in a position which suits his or her attentional style.

Different sports require different attentional focus: a hockey player needs to switch focus rapidly, but an archer does not. Players will be more effective if their attentional style suits the sport or skill. This has particular implications for youngsters as they try out different sports, as the following quote shows. It comes from Geoff Cooke, once a PE teacher and more recently Coach of the Year. Commenting on the magic of coaching, he says

> 'there is no better example than the look on a child's face when achieving in sport. I once taught a boy, with a reputation as a no-hoper, who got no respect from his school mates. I suggested he tried hammer throwing which he started as a complete novice. A year later he was Yorkshire Champion and towards the top in the whole country – his experience of sporting success completely changed him.'
>
> (From 'Supercoach', *National Coaching Foundation* Issue 3, 1997.)

If this youngster had athletic ability but a narrow internal focus, he would perform poorly in team games as they require broad-internal and external focus and contain many distractions, which leads to overload. In hammer-throwing, with no players and few crowd distractions, the tendency to narrow internal focus is an asset, not a liability, and may have been one reason for his success.

Self-talk

Self-talk refers to the conversations we have with ourselves. These conversations can help us to monitor or direct our thoughts and actions: a coach may use cue words to help a player concentrate or recall the key feature of a skill, for example 'step, swing' in a backhand tennis shot. Self-talk can also hinder our efforts.

Positive and negative self-talk

John Newcombe's description of how he took control of himself in the final against Rosewall (see p. 161) is an example of positive self-talk because it helped Newcombe focus on what was important. However if he had said to himself 'That's it, I've blown the match now', then he would have been unable to gather his resources eventually to win the match. Negative self-talk leads to frustration, anxiety, lowered effort and poor attention.

In self-talk we are interpreting events for ourselves. Missing a putt at an important point in a golf tournament is an event. As we saw under Stress (p. 110), it is how the golfer *interprets* this event which is the crucial factor, and will affect his concentration, muscle tension and motivation. How can we change self-talk from negative to positive? Two widely used strategies are described below.

- **Thought stopping**: this means stopping the negative thought as soon as it occurs. You practise stopping the thought by using a particular word or action, perhaps by saying 'stop' out loud. Then you focus on an aspect of the skill. For example, if your opponent has a very deceptive serve you might start thinking 'Where is it going to go next? I'll never get it; I missed it last time'. You practise saying 'stop' as soon as this sequence starts and instead say 'ball' to focus your attention on what is important. With practice, you can say 'stop' under your breath and eventually silently.
- **Substitution**: this means changing negative into positive thoughts so that you see the circumstances in a more positive way. Most of us have negative thoughts in particular situations; the strategy is to recast them in a positive way. For example, a referee gives a poor decision and your self-talk is 'There's no way that was off-side. That's at least the third decision that's gone against us. What chance have we got...'. If you know this happens to you, then whenever the referee gives a questionable decision you practise saying 'Right, get the ball back, take them by surprise'.

Thus, positive self-talk can improve performance by helping us to:

- remind ourselves of a key element in a new skill: 'Step, swing' in a backhand shot;
- break a bad habit: 'Stop!';

- motivate ourselves: 'Hang in there';
- concentrate: 'Watch the ball';
- reduce arousal: 'OK now, d..e..e..p breath';
- re-interpret negative events in a positive way: 'Right, let's take them by surprise'.

SELF-EFFICACY AND SELF-CONFIDENCE

Bandura (1977b) proposed that as people learn that they can master things they develop a feeling of *self-efficacy*, the expectation that they will be competent and successful in a particular task. This is not the same as self-confidence, which is more general. For example, a player may have a high level of self-efficacy on a tennis court (which will enable him or her to meet stronger opposition with a positive attitude) but not on a basketball court, which is a different circumstance. Nevertheless, self-efficacy can be seen as a specific form of self-confidence, so the two are often used interchangeably.

Bandura (1982) found that those with high levels of self-efficacy try harder and persist longer, but those low in self-efficacy give up in the face of difficulty, attribute failure to internal causes (they blame themselves) and experience greater anxiety or depression. Self-efficacy is closely linked to attributions (see p. 146) and to the need for competence (see p. 6).

Bandura suggests that *expectations* of efficacy are the major reasons for our choice of activity, the amount of effort we put into it and the degree of persistence we show – we prefer to be in situations in which we experience self-efficacy. If we are to encourage people to participate in sports and physical activities, to maintain their interest and improve performance, clearly we need to help them develop self-efficacy. In order to do so, we need to know a little more about it.

The development of self-efficacy

Bandura proposed that self-efficacy comes from four sources, as shown in Figure 6.6. These sources are:

- **past performance**: previous experiences provide information from which self-efficacy develops. Experiences of success increase self-efficacy, whereas experience of failure may reduce self-efficacy or even prevent its development. Past success is the most powerful influence on self-efficacy; once self-efficacy is established, the individual is better able to tolerate some failure. If you have beaten me three times on the squash court, you will not be very concerned at losing the fourth game. However, past failure lowers expectations for future success and reduces motivation. Thus, failure is particularly damaging to the novice, who must first develop self-efficacy in order to cope with failure. If I am new to squash, three losses on the run might deter me from ever playing a fourth game!

■ **vicarious experiences**: this means watching others successfully perform the task, and is called *modelling*. By watching others be successful, the individual approaches his or her own efforts with more confidence. If your friend watches you beat me, this increases his self-efficacy – he is more likely to think he too will beat me.

■ **verbal persuasion**: encouraging performers to think they can do the task. A team-mate who says 'Come on, you can do it' may increase her partner's self-efficacy, although persuasion does not appear to be a very powerful factor.

■ **arousal**: the way the performers interpret the arousal they feel will affect their feelings of confidence. Bandura (1977b) argues that what matters is the athlete's *interpretation* of the arousal in terms of his or her performance. Research with swimmers, cricketers and gymnasts suggest that positive perceptions of arousal are related to higher levels of confidence. However, interpreting increased pulse rate as anxiety may reduce self-efficacy. The relationship between arousal and performance is very complex, and is covered in more detail in Chapter 4.

Some of these factors were compared in the research described below.

RESEARCH
McAuley (1985)

This research compared various techniques for teaching gymnasts a dive roll mount on to the balance beam. Guiding the gymnast through the move slowly was more effective than having the gymnast watch another model perform the move. In other words, previous successful experience produced a more successful move than vicarious experience. It was also related to lower levels of anxiety than using verbal persuasion. However, these findings may be related to the type of task and skill level of the learner.

Self-efficacy and performance

Bandura proposed that these four sources of self-efficacy combine to increase expectations of success, which in turn affects performance. Thus, self-efficacy is known as the *mediating variable*: it is the link between these four sources and athletic performance. Self-efficacy is dynamic: it will vary due to these factors and how they interact together. Figure 6.6 shows this relationship in diagram form.

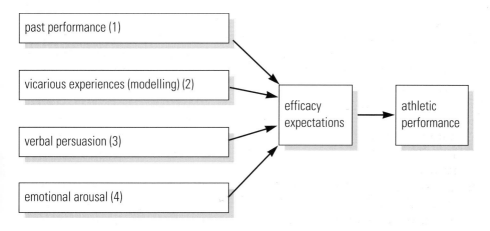

FIGURE 6.6 *Diagram showing the relationship between four sources of information, self-efficacy and performance.*

We can see that the more success a player experiences, the greater the self-efficacy and therefore the more likelihood of success. For example, David Hemery (1986) noted that Chris Evert Lloyd said that winning when young brought her self-confidence.

Self-efficacy is specific to particular tasks but also varies according to changes in the four sources just discussed. For example, a squash player may have high self-efficacy when playing against others of his ability, with the exception of one particular opponent. Perhaps he has been beaten by this player before (1) or for some reason he feels increased arousal (4) when facing this player. However, if the squash player sees *others* beat this opponent, he may gain in self-efficacy due to vicarious experience (2).

Research into self-efficacy in a team setting has produced interesting results. For example, Feltz, Bandura and Lirgg (1989) studied a hockey team throughout a season of 32 games. They found that in the first game of the season *individual* self-efficacy was more closely correlated to *team* performance than team self-efficacy. However, within eight games this had reversed because team self-efficacy was more closely correlated to team performance than individual self-efficacy. This suggests team self-efficacy may take time to develop but may become more important than individual self-efficacy, which has implications for team/group cohesion and how a coach or captain can help it develop. For more on group cohesion, see p. 121.

These are not the only factors that improve participation or performance. For example, Jourden, Bandura and Banfield (1991) showed that self-efficacy develops when athletes believe it is their own efforts (as opposed to innate ability) which lead to improved performance. Athletes who learned a motor task in the belief that performance was due to innate ability showed little interest in the activity or in developing the skill. Bandura acknowledged that factors such as having the necessary skills, setting appropriate goals, making the correct attributions and feeling mentally and physically ready also affect performance.

APPLICATION
Developing self-efficacy

A coach can use the following strategies to develop self-efficacy in players:

- Provide opportunities for players to experience success, particularly those new to the sport. This means asking them to do only that which is within their ability.
- Show (by words, actions and body language) that you have confidence in the player's ability: act confidently and encourage players to act confidently.
- Use goal setting to enable players to experience success, paying particular attention to attainable goals.
- Help players to make internal attributions for success, so they see it as due to their own efforts.
- Help players to think confidently, perhaps by using positive self-talk.
- Ensure players are well prepared, mentally and physically, for their event.
- Give players ideas for using imagery to visualise success.
- Emphasise performance goals rather than outcome goal.
- Help players interpret their arousal in a positive way.

CHAPTER SUMMARY

This chapter has reviewed ways in which sportspeople can maintain interest and improve performance in their sports. We have considered cognitive factors, such as attention or imagery, as well as ideas from learning theory, such as reinforcement. We have recognised that when participants seem to lose interest we could discover what attributions they make, in order to help them change their perceptions. At several points throughout this book we have noted that self-efficacy is a factor in maintaining participation and improving performance; many of the techniques detailed in this chapter, such as goal setting and positive self-talk, will contribute to developing self-efficacy.

REFERENCES

Adams, J.A. (1971). Closed loop theory of motor learning. *Journal of Motor Behaviour*, **3**, 111–150.

Al-Talib, N.M. (1970) Effects of consonant and dissonant role playing with high or low justification on attitude change toward physical education courses. *Research Quarterly*, **41**, 467–471.

Atkinson, J.W. (1964). *An Introduction to Motivation*. Princeton, NJ: Van Nostrand.

Baddeley, A. (1986). *Working Memory*. Oxford: Oxford University Press.

Baddeley, A. and Longman, D.J.A. (1978). The influence of length and frequency of training session on the range of learning to type. *Ergonomic*, **21**, 627–635.

Bakker, F.C., Whiting H.T.A and van der Brug, H. (1990). *Sport Psychology: Concepts and Applications*. Chichester: John Wiley & Sons.

Bandura, A. (1977a). *Social Learning Theory*. Englewood Cliffs, NJ: Pentice-Hall.

Bandura, A. (1977b). Self-efficacy: Toward a unifying theory of behavioral change. *Psychological Review*, **84**, 191–215.

Bandura, A. (1982). Self-efficacy mechanism in human agency. *American Psychologist*, **37**, 122–147.

Baron, R.S. (1986). Distraction–conflict theory: Progress and problems. In Berkowitz, L. (ed) *Advances in Experimental Social Psychology*, Vol. 19, New York: Academic Press.

Bell, G.J. and Howe, B.L. (1988). Mood state profiles and motivations of triathletes. *Journal of Sport Behavior*, **11**, 66–77.

Berkowitz, L. (1969). *Roots of Aggression*. New York: Atherton Press.

Bird, A.M. and Horn, A. (1990). Cognitive anxiety and mental errors in sport. *Journal of Sport and Exercise Psychology*, **12**, 211–216.

Bird, A.M. and Williams, J.M. (1980). A developmental-attributional analysis of sex-role stereotypes for sport performance. *Developmental Psychology*, **16**, 319–322.

Bowers, K.S. (1973). Situationalism in psychology: An analysis and a critique. *Psychological Review*, **80**, 307–336.

Bredemeier, B.J. and Shields, D.L. (1986). Athletic aggression: An issue of contextual morality. *Sociology of Sport Journal*, **3**, 15–28.

Brinker, B.P.L.M. den. (1979). Extra feedback in the learning of movements. In H. Nakken (ed) *Psychomotorische Leerprocessen (Psychomotor Learning Processes)*. Haarlem: De Vrieseborch.

Burton, D. (1988). Do anxious swimmers swim slower? Reexamining the elusive anxiety–performance relationship. *Journal of Sport and Exercise Psychology*, **10**, 45–61.

Butt, D.S. (1987) *Psychology of Sport*, 2nd edn. New York: Van Nostrand Reinhold.

Carron, A.V. (1982). Cohesiveness in sports groups: Interpretations and considerations. *Journal of Sport Psychology*, **4**, 123–138.

Cattell, R.B. (1965). *The Scientific Analysis of Personality*. Baltimore: Penguin.

Chelladurai, P. and Carron, A.V. (1978). *Leadership*. Sociology of Sport Monograph Series. Ottawa: Canadian Association for Health, Physical Education and Recreation.

Chelladurai, P. and Carron, A.V. (1983). Athletic maturity and preferred leadership. *Journal of Sport Psychology*, **5**, 371–380.

Christie, L. (1995). *To be Honest with You*. Harmondsworth: Penguin.

Coon, D. (1983). *Introduction to Psychology*, 3rd edn. St Paul, Minn: West Publishing Co.

Cooper, L. (1969). Athletics, activity, and personality: A review of the literature. *Research Quarterly*, **40**, 17–22.

Cottrell, N.B. (1968). Performance in the presence of other human beings: Mere presence, audience, and affiliation effects. In Simmell, E.C., Hoppe, R.A. and Milton, G.A. (eds) *Social Facilitation and Imitative Behaviour*, Boston: Allyn & Bacon.

Cox, R.H. (1994). *Sports Psychology: Concepts and Applications*, 3rd edn. Dubuque, IA: Wm C. Brown Communications.

Deci, E. (1975). *Intrinsic Motivation*, New York: Plenum Press.

Deci, E.L., Betley, G., Kahle, J., Abrams, L. and Porac, J. (1981). When trying to win: Competition and intrinsic motivation. *Personality and Social Psychology Bulletin*, **7**, 79–83.

Dollard, J., Doob, J., Miller, N., Mowrer, O. and Sears, R. (1939). *Frustration and Aggression*. New Haven, CT: Yale University Press.

Duke, M., Johnson, T.C. and Nowicki, S., Jr (1977). Effects of sports fitness campus experience on locus of control orientation in children, ages 6–14. *Research Quarterly*, **48**(2), 280–283.

Dweck, C. (1975). The role of expectations and attributes in the alleviation of learned helplessness. *Journal of Personality and Social Psychology*, **31**, 674–685.

Emerson, R. (1966). Mount Everest: A case study of communication feedback and sustained goal striving. *Sociometry*, **29**, 213–277.

Eysenck, H.J. (1965). *Fact and Fiction in Psychology*. Harmondsworth: Penguin.

Eysenck, H.J. and Eysenck, S.B.G. (1964). *Manual of Eysenck Personality Inventory*. London: University of London Press.

Eysenck, H.J., Nias, D.K.B. and Cox, D.N. (1982). Sport and personality. *Advances in Behaviour Research and Therapy*, **4**, 1–56.

Fazey, J. and Hardy, L. (1988). The inverted-U hypothesis: a catastrophe for sport psychology? *British Association of Sports Sciences Monograph No.1*. Leeds: The National Coaching Foundation.

Feltz, D.L., Bandura, A. and Lirgg, D.C. (1989). Perceived collective efficacy in hockey. In Kendzierski, D. (Chair) *Self-perceptions in Sport and Physical Activity: Self-efficacy and Self-image*. Symposium conducted at the meeting of the American Psychological Association, New Orleans.

Feltz, D.L., and Landers, D.M. (1983). The effects of mental practice on motor skill learning and performance: A meta-analysis. *Journal of Sport Psychology*, **5**, 25–57.

Festinger, L.A. (1957). *A Theory of Cognitive Dissonance*. New York: Harper & Row.

Fiedler, F.E. (1967) *A Theory of Leadership Effectiveness*. New York: McGraw-Hill.

Fitts, P.M. and Posner, M.I. (1967) *Human Performance*. Belmont, CA: Brooks/Cole.

Fleishman, E.A. (1964). *The Structure and Measurement of Physical Fitness*. Englewood Cliffs, NJ: Prentice-Hall.

Gill, D.L. (1980). Success–failure attributions in competitive groups: An exception to egocentrism. *Journal of Sport Psychology*, **2**, 106–114.

Gill, D.L. (1986). *Psychological Dynamics of Sport*. Champaign IL: Human Kinetics Publishers.

Gill, D.L. and Deeter, T.E. (1988). Development of the SOQ. *Research Quarterly for Exercise and Sport*, **59**, 191–202.

Hanin, Y.L. (1980). A study of anxiety in sports. In Straub, W.F. (ed.) *Sport Psychology: An Analysis of Athlete Behavior*, Ithaca, NY: Mouvement Publications.

Hemery, D. (1986). *Sporting Excellence*. Champaign, IL: Human Kinetics Publishers.

Hemphill, J.K. and Coons, A.E. (1957). Development of the leader behavior description questionnaire. In Stodgill, R.M. and Coons, A.E. (eds) *Leader Behavior: Its Description and Measurement*. Columbus: Ohio State University Press.

Hick, W.E. (1952). On the rate of gain of information. *Quarterly Journal of Experimental Psychology*, **4**, 11–26.

Hollander, E.P. (1971). *Principles and Methods of Social Psychology*, 2nd edn. New York: Oxford University Press.

Horn, T. and Glenn, S. (1988). The relationship between athletes' psychological characteristics and their preference for particular coaching behaviors. Paper presented at the meeting of the North American Society for the Psychology of Sport and Physical Activity, Knoxville, Tennessee, USA.

Hovland, C.I., Janis, I.L. and Kelley, H.H. (1953). *Communication and Persuasion*. New Haven: Yale University Press.

Hull, C.L. (1951). *Essentials of Behavior*. New Haven: Yale University Press.

Husman, B.F. and Silva, J.M. (1984). Aggression in sport: Definitional and theoretical considerations. In Silva, J.M. and Weinberg, R.S. (eds) *Psychological Foundations of Sport*. Champaign, IL: Human Kinetics Publishers.

Johnson, D.W. and Johnson, R. (1985). Classroom conflict: Controversy over debate in learning groups. *American Educational Research Journal*, **22**, 237–256.

Jones, J.G. and Hardy, L. (1990). *Stress and Performance in Sport*. Chichester: John Wiley & Sons.

Jourden, F.J., Bandura, A. and Banfield, J.T. (1991). The impact of conceptions of ability on self-regulatory factors and motor skill acquisition. *Journal of Sport and Exercise Psychology*, **13**, 213–226.

Kahneman, D. (1973). *Attention and Effort*. Englewood Cliffs, NJ: Prentice Hall.

Knapp, B. (1963). *Skills in Sport*. London: Routledge Kegan Paul.

Kremer, J. and Scully, D. (1994). *Psychology in Sport*. London: Taylor & Francis.

Kroll, W. and Crenshaw, W. (1970). Multivariate personality profile analysis of four athletic groups. In Kenyon, G.S. (ed) *Contemporary Psychology of Sport: Second International Congress of Sport Psychology*. Chicago: The Athletic Institute.

Lacey, J.J. (1967). Somatic response patterning and stress: Some revisions of activation theory. In Appley, M.H. and Trumbell, R. (eds) *Psychological Stress: Issues in Research*. New York: Appleton-Century-Crofts.

Landers, D.M. and Landers, D.M. (1973). Teacher versus peer models: Effects of model's presence and performance level on motor behavior. *Journal of Motor Behavior*, **5**, 129–139.

Latané, B., Harkins, S.G. Williams, K.D. (1980). *Many Hands make Light Work: Social Loafing as a Social Disease*. Unpublished manuscript. Columbus: Ohio State University.

Lazarus, R.S. and Folkman, S. (1984). *Stress, Appraisal and Coping*. New York: Springer.

Lenney, E. (1977). Women's self-confidence in achievement situations. *Psychological Bulletin*, **84**, 1–13.

Lepper, M.R. and Greene, D. (1975). Turning play into work: Effect of adult surveillance and extrinsic rewards on children's intrinsic motivation. *Journal of Personality and Social Psychology*, **31**, 479–486.

Lewin, K., Lippitt, R. and White, R. (1939). Patterns of aggressive behaviour in experimentally created 'social climates'. *Journal of Social Psychology*, **10**, 271–299.

Likert, R.A. (1932). A technique for the measurement of attitudes. *Archives of Psychology*, **140**, 1–55.

Lowe, R. (1973). *Stress, Arousal and Task Performance of Little League Baseball Players*. Unpublished doctoral dissertation, University of Illinois, Urbana-Champaign.

Marteniuk, R.G. (1976). *Information Processing in Motor Skills*. New York: Holt, Rinehart & Winston.

Martens, R.A. (1976). *Competitiveness and sport*. Paper presented at the International Congress of Physical Activity Sciences, Quebec City.

Martens, R.A. (1977). *Sport Competition Anxiety Test*. Champaign, IL: Human Kinetics Publishers.

Martens, R.A., Vealey, R.S. and Burton, D. (1990). *Competitive Anxiety in Sport*. Champaign, IL: Human Kinetics Publishers.

Maslow, A. (1954). *Motivation and Personality*. New York: Harper & Row.

McAuley, E. (1985). Modelling and self-efficacy: A test of Bandura's model. *Journal of Sport Psychology*, **7**, 283–295.

McNair, D.M., Lorr, M. and Droppleman, L.F. (1971). *Profile of Mood States Manual*. San Diego: Educational and Industrial Testing Service.

Miller, N.E. (1941). The frustration–aggression hypothesis. *Psychological Review*, **48**, 337–342.

Mischel, W. (1968). *Personality and Adjustment*. New York: Wiley.

Morgan, W.P. (1979). Prediction of performance in athletics. In Klavora, P. and Daniel, J.V. (eds) *Coach, Athlete, and the Sport Psychologist*. Champaign, IL: Human Kinetics Publishers.

Morgan, W.P., Brown. D.R., Raglin, J.S., O'Connor, P.J. and Ellickson, K.A. (1987a). Psychological monitoring of overtraining and staleness. *British Journal of Sports Medicine*, **21**(3), 107–114.

Morgan, W.P. and Costill, D.L. (1972). Psychological characteristics of the marathon runner. *Journal of Sports Medicine and Physical Fitness*, **12**, 42–46.

Morgan, W.P., O'Connor, P.J., Sparling, P.B. and Pate, R.R. (1987b). Psychological characterization of the elite female distance runner. *International Journal of Sports Medicine*, **8**, 124–131.

Mosston, M. and Ashworth, S. (1986). *Teaching Physical Education*. Columbus, Ohio: Merrill Publishing Co.

Nideffer, R.M. (1985). *Athlete's Guide to Mental Training*. Champaign, IL: Human Kinetics Publishers.

Nideffer, R.M. (1976a). *The Inner Athlete: Mind plus Muscle for Winning*. New York: Thomas T. Crowell Company.

Nideffer, R.M. (1976b). Test of attentional and interpersonal style. *Journal of Personality and Social Psychology*, **34**, 394–404.

Nisbett, R.E., Caputo, C., Legant, P. and Maracek, J. (1973). Behaviour as seen by the actor and as seen by the observer. *Journal of Personality and Social Psychology*, **27**, 154–165.

Orlick, T. (1978). *Winning Through Cooperation*. Washington, DC: Hawkins.

Osgood, C.E., Suci, G.J. and Tannenbaum, P.H. (1957). *The Measurement of Meaning*. Urbana, IL: University of Illinois Press.

Oxendine, J.B. (1970). Emotional arousal and motor performance. *Quest*, **13**, 23–30.

Rogan, J. (1989). *The Football Managers*. London: Macdonald and Co.

Rotter, J.B. (1966). Generalised expectancies for internal versus external control of reinforcement. *Psychological Monographs*, **80** (1 Whole No. 609).

Rotter, J.B. (1971). External control and internal control. *Psychology Today*, **5**(1), 37–42, 58–59.

Schachter, S. and Singer, J.E. (1962). Cognitive, social and physiological determinants of emotional state. *Psychological Review*, **69**, 379–399.

Schmidt, R.A. (1975). A schema theory of discrete motor skill learning. *Psychological Review*, **82**, 225–260.

Seligman, M.E.P. (1975). *Helplessness: on Depression, Development, and Death*. San Francisco: W.H. Freeman.

Singer, R.N. (1980). *Motor Learning and Human Performance*, 3rd edn. New York: Macmillan.

Skinner, B.F. (1938). *The Behavior of Organisms*. New York. Appleton-Century-Crofts.

Smith, R.E. (1980). A cognitive–affective approach to stress management training for athletes. In Nadeau, C.H. (ed) *Psychology of Motor Behavior and Sport, 1979*, pp. 54–72. Champaign, IL: Human Kinetics Publishers.

Smith, R.E., Smoll, F.L. and Curtis, B. (1979). Coach effectiveness training: A cognitive–behavioural approach to enhancing relationship skills in youth sports coaches. *Journal of Sport Psychology*, **1**, 59–75.

Spence, K.W. (1956). *Behaviour Theory and Conditioning*. New Haven: Yale University Press.

Spielberger, C.D. (1966). *Anxiety and Behavior*. New York: Academic Press.

Steiner, I.D. (1972). *Group Processes and Productivity*. New York: Academic Press.

Suinn, R.M. (1980). Body thinking: Psychology for Olympic champs. In Suinn, R.M. (ed) *Psychology in Sports: Methods and Applications*. Minneapolis: Burgess Publishing Company.

Suinn, R.M. (1983). Imagery and sports. In Sheikh A.A. (ed) *Imagery: Current Theory, Research, and Application*. New York: Wiley.

Tajfel, H. (ed) (1978). *Differentiation Between Social Groups: Studies in the Social Psychology of Intergroup Relations*. London: Academic Press.

Thorndike, E.L. (1931). *Human Learning*. New York: Appleton-Century-Crofts.

Thurstone, L.L. (1931). The measurement of social attitudes. *Journal of Abnormal and Social Psychology*, **26**, 249–269.

Triandis, H.C. (1971). *Attitude and Attitude Change*. New York: Wiley.

Triplett, N. (1898). The dynamogenic factors in pacemaking and competition. *American Journal of Psychology*, **9**, 507–33.

Tuckman, B.W. (1965). Developmental sequences in small groups. *Psychological Bulletin*, **63**, 384–399.

Veroff, J. (1969). Social comparison and the development of achievement motivation. In Smith, C.P. (ed) *Achievement-related Motives in Children*. New York: Russell Sage Foundation.

Wein, H. (1985). *The Science of Hockey*. London: Pelham Books.

Weinberg, R.S. and Gould, D. (1995). *Foundations of Sport and Exercise Psychology*. Champaign, IL: Human Kinetics Publishers.

Weinberg, R.S. and Hunt, U.V. (1976). The relationship between anxiety, motor performance, and electromyography. *Journal of Motor Behaviour*, **8**, 219–224.

Weiner, B. (1972). *Theories of Motivation: From Mechanism to Cognition*. Chicago: Rand McNally.

Weiner, B. (1979). A theory of motivation for some classroom experiences. *Journal of Educational Psychology*, 71, 3–25.

Welford, A.T. (1952). The psychological refractory period and the timing of high-speed performance – a review and a theory. *British Journal of Psychology*, **43**, 2–19.

White, R.W. (1959). Motivation reconsidered: The concept of competence. *Psychological Review*, **66**, 297–333.

Whiting, H.T.A. (1975). *Concepts in Skill Learning*. London: Lepus Books.

Williams, L.R.T. and Parkin, W.A. (1980). Personality profiles of three hockey groups. *International Journal of Sports Psychology*, **11**, 113–120.

Zajonc, R.B. (1965). Social facilitation. *Science*, **149**, 269–274.

Zander, A. (1975). Motivation and performance of sports groups. In Landers, D.M. (ed) *Psychology of Sport and Motor Behavior II*. University Park, PA: Pennsylvania State University Press.

Ziegler, S.G. (1978). An overview of anxiety management strategies in sport. In Straub, W.F. (ed) *Sports Psychology: An Analysis of Athlete Behaviour*. Ithaca, NY: Mouvement Publications.

INDEX

180

PICTURE CREDITS

The author and publisher would like to thank the following copyright holders for their permission to use material in this book:

Action Plus for Figures 1.2 (p.4), 1.3(b) (p.8), 1.4 (right) (p.12), 1.8 (p.21), 2.2 (p.37), 2.7 (p.46), 2.13 (p.58), 3.3 (p.72), 3.5 (p.77), 3.7 (p.82), 5.1 (p.119), 5.2 (p.121), 5.6 (p.138), 6.2 (p.149) and 6.5 (p.162); **All sport** for Figures 1.4 (p.12), 3.2 (p.70), 5.3 (p.129) and 6.1 (p.145); **Associated Press** for Figure 2.1 (p.33); **Patrick Eager** for Figure 2.6 (p.43) and 6.3 (p.151); **Sally and Richard Greenhill** for Figure 1.3(a) (p.8); **Human Kinetics** for Figures 4.6 (p.100) and 4.8 (p.103); **David Mitchelson, Charnwood Dynamics Ltd** for Figure 2.11 (p.53); **The National Coaching Foundation** for Figure 3.8 (p.88) from the *Working with Children Introductory Study Pack 7* (1989); **Oxford University Press** for Figure 1.5 (p.13) from E.P. Hollander (1976) *Principles and Methods of Social Psychology*, 3rd Ed.

Every effort has been made to obtain necessary permission with reference to copyright material. The publishers apologise if inadvertently any sources remain unacknowledged and will be glad to make the necessary arrangements at the earliest opportunity.

Further titles in the *Applying Psychology to...* series are available from Hodder & Stoughton.

0340 64756 6 **Applying Psychology to Health** by Philip Banyard £7.99 ☐

0340 64392 7 **Applying Psychology to Early Child Development** £7.99 ☐

0340 64758 2 **Applying Psychology to Organisations** by Sheila Heyward £7.99 ☐

0340 64329 3 **Applying Psychology to Crime** by Julie Harrower £8.99 ☐

0340 64757 4 **Applying Psychology to the Environment** by Susan Cave £8.99 ☐

0340 64760 4 **Applying Psychology to Sport** by Barbara Woods £7.99 ☐

For full details of this series, please call Kerry Grieves at Hodder & Stoughton on 0171 873 6246.

All Hodder & Stoughton *Educational* books are available at your local bookshop, or can be ordered direct from the publisher. Just tick the titles you would like and complete the details below. Prices and availability are subject to change without prior notice.

Please enclose a cheque or postal order made payable to *Bookpoint Limited*, and send to: Hodder & Stoughton *Educational*, 39 Milton Park, Abingdon, Oxon OX14 4TD, UK. EMail address: orders@bookpoint.co.uk

Buy four books from the selection above and get free postage and packaging. Just send a cheque or postal order to the value of the total cover price of four books. Alternatively, if you wish to buy fewer than four books the following postage and packaging applies:

UK & BFPO £4.30 for one book; £6.30 for two books; £8.30 for three books

Overseas and Eire: £4.80 for one book; £7.10 for two or three books (surface mail)

If you would like to pay by credit card, our centre team would be delighted to take your order by telephone. Our direct line (44) 01235 400414 (lines open 9.00 am–6.00 pm, Monday to Saturday, with a 24 hour answering service). Alternatively you can send a fax to (44) 01235 400454.

Title_____ First name_____ Surname_____

Address _____

_____

_____

Postcode _____ Daytime telephone no. _____

If you would prefer to pay by credit card, please complete:

Please debit my Master Card / Access / Diner's Card / American Express (delete as applicable)

Card number ☐☐☐☐ ☐☐☐☐ ☐☐☐☐ ☐☐☐☐

Expiry date _____ Signature _____

If you would not like to receive further information on our products, please tick the box ☐.